The Arts

FRIDA KAHLO

rourke biographies

The Arts

FRIDA KAHLO

by
JANE ANDERSON JONES

Rourke Publications, Inc.
Vero Beach, Florida 32964

∞ The paper used in this book conforms to the American
National Standard for Permanence of Paper for Printed
Library Materials, Z39.48-1984.

Library of Congress Cataloging-in-Publication Data
Jones, Jane Anderson, 1948-
    Frida Kahlo / written by Jane Anderson Jones.
    p.   cm. — (Rourke biographies. The arts)
    Includes bibliographical references and index.
    Summary: Discusses the life and work of Mexican
painter Frida Kahlo, her tempestuous marriage to Diego
Rivera, and her international reputation.
    ISBN 0-86625-485-4 (alk. paper)
    1. Kahlo, Frida, 1907-1954—Juvenile literature.   2.
Painters—Mexico—Biography—Juvenile literature.   [1.
Kahlo, Frida, 1907-1954.   2. Artists.]   I. Title.   II. Series.
ND259.K33J65   1993
759.972—dc20
[B]   92-44758
                                                           CIP
                                                           AC

Contents

Color Illustrations

The Arts

FRIDA KAHLO

Chapter 1

Portrait of the Artist as a Mexican

Frida Kahlo lived from 1907 to 1954. When she died, a few days after her forty-seventh birthday, she left behind at least 143 paintings that helped to change the way critics and the public judge women artists. In her paintings, Kahlo explored her Mexican heritage while she defined her own being. Fifty-five of her paintings are self-portraits: portraits in which, sometimes shockingly and always vividly, she constructs her own reality. Kahlo's paintings proclaim the woman as artist and as definer of her own life.

Although Kahlo was born in 1907, she claimed the year 1910 as the year of her birth. Frida was not attempting to seem younger: When she "decided" to be born in 1910, she was still a teenager, who well might want to add a year or two to her age. The Mexican Revolution began in 1910, and Frida identified her own beginnings with the beginning of the Revolution. The Revolution, lasting from 1910 to 1920, saw the end of the long dictatorship of General Porfirio Díaz, and with it a new interest in Mexican culture. Frida grew up at the center of this swirl of change, and she proudly claimed the richness of her multicultural heritage.

Like many Mexicans, Frida's heritage was ethnically mixed. Her mother's family was Mexican, connected to both the colonial and Indian (Native Mexican) histories of the country: Her Créole grandmother was the daughter of a Spanish general, and her photographer grandfather was of Indian descent. Her father had emigrated to Mexico from

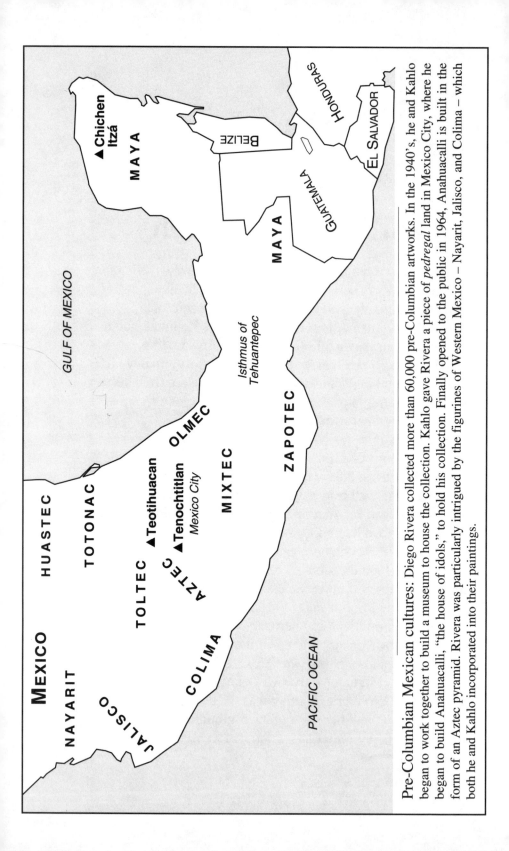

MEXICO

NAYARIT

JALISCO

HUASTEC

TOTONAC

TOLTEC

AZTEC

COLIMA

▲Teotihuacan

▲Tenochtitlan
Mexico City

OLMEC

MIXTEC

ZAPOTEC

GULF OF MEXICO

Isthmus of Tehuantepec

PACIFIC OCEAN

MAYA

▲Chichen Itzá

BELIZE

GUATEMALA

HONDURAS

EL SALVADOR

MAYA

Pre-Columbian Mexican cultures: Diego Rivera collected more than 60,000 pre-Columbian artworks. In the 1940's, he and Kahlo began to work together to build a museum to house the collection. Kahlo gave Rivera a piece of *pedregal* land in Mexico City, where he began to build Anahuacalli, "the house of idols," to hold his collection. Finally opened to the public in 1964, Anahuacalli is built in the form of an Aztec pyramid. Rivera was particularly intrigued by the figurines of Western Mexico – Nayarit, Jalisco, and Colima – which both he and Kahlo incorporated into their paintings.

Baden-Baden, Germany, where his Hungarian-Jewish parents
had settled.

One of Frida's earliest memories was of a street battle
during the Revolution between the followers of the
revolutionary Emiliano Zapata and the provisional government
troops of Venustiano Carranza:

> I witnessed with my own eyes Zapata's peasants battle against the
> Carrancistas. My situation was very clear. My mother opened the
> windows on Allende Street. She gave access to the Zapatistas, seeing
> to it that the wounded and hungry jumped from the windows of my
> house in the "living room." She cured them and gave them thick
> tortillas, the only food that could be obtained in Coyoacán in those
> days. . . .[1]

Frida and her sisters, carried away by the excitement of the
Revolution, sang Zapatista *corridos* (ballads). They were not
the only ones carried away by the excitement.

The Mexicanidad Movement

The Mexicanidad movement in the arts began as
intellectuals and artists attached themselves to various
revolutionary leaders, first advising them and later recording
their deeds. When the fighting finally ended in 1920, a need to
affirm their Mexican heritage played a large role in the efforts
to create a modern Mexico. The government funded the
excavation and restoration of archaeological sites and
commissioned painters to decorate the walls of public
buildings with murals. The only requirement of the painters
was that their subjects be Mexican. The native myths and
history of Mexico—from its days of Mayan and Aztec glory
through the horrors of the Spanish Conquest to the wars for
independence and revolutionary change—were brought to life
in monumental display.

Frida grew up in the midst of the artistic ferment. When she was a student at the National Preparatory School, Diego Rivera (her future husband) was painting murals on its walls. As a young woman Frida moved among the intellectual and artistic society of Mexico City. Her paintings reflect the nourishment and inspiration that she found in her Mexican heritage.

Kahlo's Mexican Heritage

One project that involved Kahlo throughout much of her career was an autobiography of her life in paintings. The works illustrating her childhood from this series include *My Birth* (1932), *My Grandparents, My Parents, and I* (1936), *My Nurse and I* (1937), *Four Inhabitants of Mexico* (1938), *Girl with Death Mask* (1938), and *They Ask for Planes and Are Given Straw Wings* (1938). All use Mexican imagery and adapt traditional forms in inventive and sometimes startling images.

My Birth combines forms from Aztec statues, Roman Catholic devotional art, and the popular *ex-voto* (or *retablo*) tin paintings, which depict supernatural events. The Aztec goddess of childbirth, Tlazoltéotl, carved in the act of childbirth, is Kahlo's model for this image of her own birth, but she transforms the image into a shocking and graphic presentation of the infant Frida's head emerging from the womb, dripping with blood. In Aztec imagery, a woman in childbirth represents the birth of a new era, perhaps the era that Frida claimed when she identified her birth date with the beginning of the Mexican Revolution. Her memories of her childhood home create the setting of the painting: her mother's bed, in which Frida was born, with a painting of the Virgin of Sorrows above it. Like the traditional *retablo*, *My Birth* is small (12½ by 14 inches), painted on sheet metal, and depicts both a miraculous event and a divine being. This combination of contrasting Mexican traditions is typical of Kahlo's work, placing it within the larger heritage but claiming her own particular vision.

In *My Nurse and I*, Kahlo paints herself with an adult head in the arms of an Indian wet-nurse who nourishes her with the

The goddess Tlazoltéotl, giving birth. (Dumbarton Oaks
Research Library and Collections, Washington, D.C.)

This sixteenth-century stone figure (above) was sculpted, polished, and originally adorned with garnets by the Aztec Indians shortly before the Spanish Conquest. From the time Hernán Cortés conquered the Aztec Empire in 1519 until 1810, Spain ruled Mexico. Even after the War for Independence, Spanish standards were still the norm for Mexican culture and art. Under Spanish rule, Mexico had been part of what was called New Spain, and rigid class distinctions were maintained. At the top of the social and political ladder were the peninsulares, *those born in Spain who had been sent to Mexico to hold the highest positions in both the government and the Roman Catholic church. Beneath them were the* criollos, *or Créoles, who were of pure European descent but had been born and reared in New Spain; they were never allowed to attain significant power, and the resentment of the Créoles against colonial rule was a major force in the move for independence. The native Indian populations were of Olmec, Teotihuacáno, Mayan, Toltec, Chichimeca, and Aztec descent. In addition were African Americans who had been brought to Mexico as slaves. Mestizos, those of mixed heritage, were the fastest-growing population at the time of the War for Independence and the Mexican Revolution. Although the ancient civilizations of Mexico produced some of the most sophisticated and intriguing art and architecture of the world, it was not until the Mexican Revolution that a reclaiming of the Mexican heritage began to take place.*

milk of Kahlo's ancestral forebears. Again, Kahlo used a
pre-Columbian statue (a statue from the period before
Christopher Columbus and the Europeans came to the
Americas) as the model for positioning the nurse and child.
This statue is from the Mexican state of Jalisco (*haléescoh*).
The Jalisco statue's breasts are decorated with plant patterns,
so Frida's nurse suckles the infant-adult from a breast whose
engorged veins resemble flowering plants. The veins in the
leaf behind the figures echo those in the nurse's breast and
suggest the connection between human life and nature. The
face of the nurse is hidden behind a stone mask from the
Teotihuacán (*tayohteewahcán*) culture because the adult Kahlo
cannot remember the face of her nurse. The representation of
nurse and child is not a tender one; the nurse holds out the
child almost as a sacrificial victim and the Teotihuacán mask is
terrifying. Kahlo was not at all sentimental about her Indian
heritage. She understood the cruel and bloody nature of the
human sacrifices the Aztecs performed to ensure the
continuation of life.

Kahlo's mixed feelings about the nurturing yet destructive
quality of Mexican life can also be seen in *Four Inhabitants of
Mexico*. In this painting, Frida as a small child is sitting in the
middle of the plaza of her hometown, Coyoacán. She painted
an empty plaza, she said, "because too much revolution has
left Mexico empty."[2] The painting was originally called *The
Square Is Theirs*; "they" are four figures of Mexican folk
art—a Judas (*hóodas*) figure wrapped in firecrackers, a clay
skeleton called a *calavera*, a pregnant pre-Columbian statue
with broken feet, and a straw horse and rider. The child seems
lost, staring at these fragile representations of Mexican culture.
Similar firecracker-draped Judas figures, usually made of
papier-mâché, were exploded on Holy Saturday (the day
before Easter) to celebrate the triumph of good over evil. The
pre-Columbian statue represents the condition of the Indian

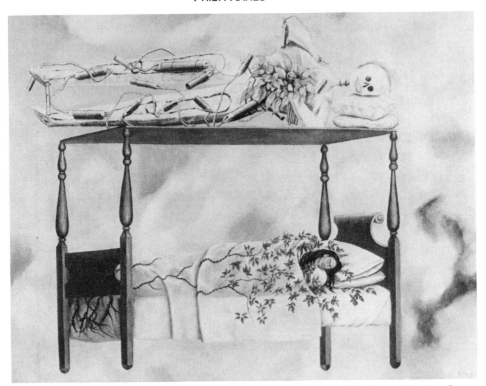

The Dream (1940): *All of Latin America takes the opportunity of the Day of the Dead to laugh at death. Picnics are held in cemeteries with special treats such as sugar skulls and skeleton cookies. During the fiesta, people dress as skeletons, skulls, or black-hooded figures. Kahlo, embracing death in order to confront her fear, played with its images. She kept a cardboard skeleton on the canopy above her bed and often dressed it in her clothes.* (Reproduction authorized by National Institute of Fine Arts and Literature, Mexico City)

population, broken yet pregnant with life. The skeleton *calavera*, a toy with which Mexican children played on November 1, the Day of the Dead, appears and reappears throughout Kahlo's paintings; for her it signified death, "very gay, a joke."[3] The straw toy represents the Mexican peasantry; Kahlo said that she included this figure "because he is weak, and at the same time has such elegance and is so easy to destroy."[4]

By putting herself in the middle of the square, Kahlo seems to be making herself the fifth inhabitant of Mexico. Why did she identify herself with these fragile and easily destroyed figures? The child is bewildered by these images, but the adult artist came to know the fragility of her own life intimately.

Kahlo's Contribution to Mexican Art

Kahlo produced small easel paintings during the period when most Mexican artists were painting huge, monumental murals. While the muralists were telling the stories of Mexico's past on the walls of public buildings for all to read, Kahlo was tapping into a lyrical vein that expressed Mexican spiritual life through her own individual lens. The muralists' work can be compared to long novels of Mexican life. Kahlo's work, by contrast, might be compared to poetry. The muralists' paintings reach outward to the viewers; Kahlo's confront the viewers and invite them in.

Frida Kahlo's important contribution to the understanding of Mexico's culture and to the wealth of its artistic heritage was recognized by the Mexican government in 1984 when it declared her work as part of the national patrimony—that is, work of "unquestioned aesthetic value and . . . unanimous recognition within the national artistic community."[5] Her work is not to be sold without the permission of the government and never to be permanently removed from the country.

Chapter 2

Childhood in Coyoacán

Frida and her father often took walks in the parks of Coyoacán, the suburb of Mexico City where Frida's father had built a house for his family. Frida loved to collect insects and plants, which they would take home to inspect under her father's microscope. Her father often carried a camera with him, for he was a professional photographer.

Usually the little girl felt protected when she held her father's hand, but sometimes she became the protector. Suddenly her father would fall, struck by an attack of epilepsy. This disease of the brain causes seizures that result in a loss of consciousness. Frida had learned what to do: She made sure that he inhaled alcohol or ether to help him regain consciousness. She guarded his precious camera so that it would not be stolen until her father was once again able to walk. Then they would continue their explorations.

Family Portrait

Magdalena Carmen Frida Kahlo y Calderón, called Frida by her family, was born on July 6, 1907. She was the third child of Matilde Calderón and Guillermo Kahlo. Matilde was the second wife of Guillermo Kahlo. His first wife had died during childbirth when their second daughter was born. Not long afterward he married Matilde, with whom he had been working in a jewelry store. Matilde and Guillermo had four daughters. Frida's two older sisters, Matilde (nicknamed "Matita") and Adriana, helped to care for Frida and her younger sister, Cristina, who was born a year after Frida. María Luisa and Margarita—Frida's two half-sisters, daughters of Guillermo's first marriage—only visited occasionally from the convent in which they were being reared. The Kahlo family lived at 247 Londres Street in Coyoacán, a suburb of Mexico City. Guillermo Kahlo had had the house built in 1904 for his growing family. He was a prosperous photographer with an important commission from the Mexican government, then headed by Porfirio Díaz, to photograph the famous buildings of Mexico as part of the centennial

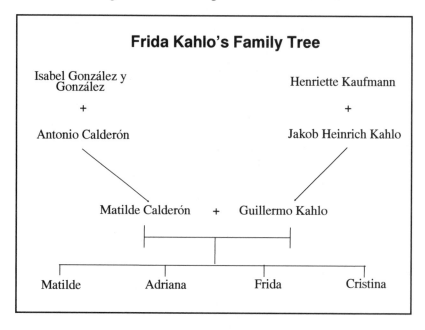

Frida Kahlo's Family Tree

Isabel González y González

Henriette Kaufmann

+

+

Antonio Calderón

Jakob Heinrich Kahlo

Matilde Calderón + Guillermo Kahlo

Matilde   Adriana   Frida   Cristina

celebration of Mexican independence. Unfortunately, when President Díaz was overthrown during the Revolution, Guillermo lost much of his business, and financial difficulties beset the family. Although they had to mortgage the house and take in boarders, the family managed to survive, partly because Frida's mother was a careful manager. Frida, who called her *mi Jefe* (my Chief), said of her mother, "She did not know how to read or write. She only knew how to count money."[6]

In her painting entitled *My Grandparents, My Parents, and I*, Kahlo painted an image of herself firmly in the middle of the patio of her Coyoacán house, surrounded by her ancestors. Frida here is a happy two-year-old who holds the images of her parents and grandparents on red ribbons—as if they were balloons floating above her head. The figures of her mother and father were painted from their wedding picture, but Kahlo added a second portrait of herself as a six-month-old fetus atop her mother's wedding dress, and just below the figure of her mother, she included a third image of her own conception as

Guillermo Kahlo, Frida's father, c. 1907. (Cenidap Archive)

Matilde Calderón de Kahlo, Frida's mother, 1926. (Cenidap Archive)

her father's sperm fertilizes her mother's egg. This is a picture of a child secure in her position at the center of her own universe.

Frida's maternal grandparents, the Indian photographer Antonio Calderón and his wife Isabel González y González, float above the *pedregal*, the rocky volcanic landscape of Mexico. Her paternal grandparents, Jakob Heinrich Kahlo and Henriette Kaufmann Kahlo, float above the sea over which Frida's father had sailed to get to Mexico.

It is apparent from this family portrait that Frida inherited physical as well as cultural traits from both sides of her family. Her high cheekbones and dark complexion were inherited from her Indian grandfather. The heavy, joined eyebrows, which Kahlo usually painted in her self-portraits, are the legacy of her father's mother. Frida herself said that she had inherited her mother's body and her father's eyes. The gazes of her father and his father reveal the intensity with which both Guillermo Kahlo and his daughter, Frida, would observe their world.

The Good Daughter

Wilhelm Kahlo was a promising student at the University of Nuremberg when he sustained brain injuries from a fall. He would suffer from epileptic seizures for the rest of his life. When Wilhelm was nineteen, his father, a jeweler and dealer in photographic supplies, agreed to finance his emigration to Mexico. On his arrival, Wilhelm translated his first name into the Hispanic equivalent, Guillermo (*geeairmoh*). He never returned to Europe. Guillermo Kahlo was a man of few words, but those few words were always keenly observant and often ironically funny. He preferred photographing buildings to taking pictures of people because, he claimed, he did not wish to improve upon what God had made ugly.

Frida was her father's favorite child; he felt she was the most intelligent of his daughters and thought that she was the most like himself. He taught her first to use a microscope to examine insects and plants and then to use a camera and to develop her film. As she grew older, she became his studio assistant, retouching and coloring her father's photographs. This early training in her father's photography laboratory taught her to be meticulous and to pay careful attention to details.

Frida and her father also shared the sufferings of physical disabilities. When Frida was six or seven years old, she contracted polio and was housebound for nine months. After her illness, her father encouraged her to make up for her skinny right leg and slight limp by climbing trees, rowing, and bicycling. Later, when she became her father's assistant, she accompanied him on photography excursions and helped him get through his epileptic attacks. The bond between father and daughter was a strong one: "My childhood was marvelous because although my father was a sick man, . . . he was an immense example to me of tenderness, of work, . . . and above all, of understanding my problems."[7]

In 1951, ten years after her father's death, Kahlo painted *Portrait of Don Guillermo Kahlo*. She painted her father as if he were posing for the camera, but she included the camera that made him the country's first official photographer. Inscribed on the scroll beneath his portrait, Kahlo wrote:

> I painted my father, Wilhelm Kahlo of Hungarian-German origin, artist-photographer by profession, in character generous, intelligent and fine, valiant because he suffered for sixty years with epilepsy, but he never stopped working and he fought against Hitler. With adoration. His daughter Frida Kahlo.[8]

The Rebel

Frida's mother, Matilde, was both very beautiful and a very devout Catholic. She insisted that her young daughters attend church every day and tried to instill in them the piety that was so important to her. Frida and her younger sister Cristina resisted:

> My mother was hysterical about religion. We had to pray before meals. While the others concentrated on their inner selves, Cristi and I would look at each other, forcing ourselves not to laugh.[9]

Later, when the two were sent to catechism class to prepare for their first communion, they played hooky and stole fruit from a nearby orchard.

Frida teased and tormented both her sisters and her parents.

She even called her father "Herr Kahlo" when his German methodicalness overtook his better nature. Perhaps the most serious prank Frida pulled was when she helped her fifteen-year-old sister Matita run away to Veracruz with her boyfriend Paco. Frida was seven at the time and opened and closed the balcony window behind her sister so it would appear that nothing had happened.

Frida's mother was furious and unforgiving. Guillermo was distraught, fearing that they would never find their daughter again, but he was helpless in the face of his wife's anger. Frida eventually tracked down her sister in Mexico City, where she and Paco lived happily. Frida could not, however, persuade her mother to see them. It would not be until twelve years after Matita had escaped that her mother would allow her back into the family home.

This childhood episode of familial discord colored Frida's perceptions of conventional morality. She continued to rebel against her mother's expectations for a young Mexican girl, which included early marriage, motherhood, and a family. In 1922, when she was fifteen, Frida's father insisted that she be allowed to attend the National Preparatory School in Mexico City.

Chapter 3

The National Preparatory School

The mischievous young girl stood behind a pillar in the National Preparatory School's auditorium and loudly whispered out to Mexico's most famous painter: "Hey, Diego, here comes Nahui." Diego Rivera was painting one of the first murals of the great modern Mexican mural revival, and his mistress, Lupe Marín, who often came to watch him paint, was jealous of his beautiful young models, especially Nahui Olín.

Frida, at fifteen, loved to tease the thirty-six-year-old painter, who had just returned from Paris to lend his talents to the rebuilding of Mexico after the Revolution. She hid in the shadows of the auditorium, amused by the procession of beautiful women Rivera painted and flirted with, and she often tried to upset the deliberate calm of the monstrous artist. Once she soaped the steps of the stage, hoping to see him go sprawling, but Rivera's heavy-footed and deliberate gait saved him.

In his autobiography, *My Art, My Life* (1960), Diego Rivera remembered his first encounter with the young student who would become his wife seven years later.

One night as Rivera was painting on the scaffold and Lupe Marín was sitting below weaving in the auditorium, Frida burst through the auditorium door and asked the painter if she could watch him paint. Rivera agreed, but the girl's presence soon began to annoy Lupe, who started to insult Frida. Frida paid no attention to the woman's insults until Lupe stood right in front of her and tried to intimidate her with a fierce stare. Frida

1942: Frida at the "blue cube," her portion of the house she and Diego shared in Mexico City. (Cenidap Archive)

stared right back until Lupe finally smiled and said to Diego, "Look at that girl! Small as she is, she does not fear a tall, strong woman like me. I really like her."[10]

Frida had a schoolgirl's crush on the famous painter and told her girlfriends that she intended to have Diego's baby someday. Her friends were horrified because they thought that Rivera was fat and ugly. Although she nicknamed him *Panzón* (fat-belly), Frida was captivated by the wise and gentle quality of the man. He awakened a maternal instinct in the girl—she even declared that she wanted to bathe him and clean him. Yet as fascinated as she was by *El Maestro* ("master" or "teacher"), Frida did not waste her time mooning over an impossible relationship.

She was far too involved with her own gang, especially its acknowledged leader, Alejandro Gómez Arias, who was Frida's boyfriend. The group of seven boys and two girls, known as *Las Cachuchas* because of the caps they wore, was notorious at the National Preparatory School for their pranks and their irreverent wit. Frida, one of the group's ringleaders, was always devising ways to upset the school's officials. Once, she and the other Cachuchas rode a donkey through the halls; another time they set off fireworks outside a classroom, causing a window to shatter its glass over a lecturing professor. They cut classes when they thought the teachers were dull or ill-prepared, and they set small fires under the scaffolds of the painters who were decorating the walls of the school with murals. The director of the school tried to expel Frida, but she appealed in person to Mexico's minister of education, José Vasconcelos. He was impressed with her academic record and her personality, and he ordered the director to reinstate her as a student, telling him, "If you can't manage a little girl like that, you are not fit to be director of such an institution."[11]

The Cachuchas were not simply troublemakers, however.

They were among the brightest of the student body—they read
widely, challenging one another to discover better books and
finish them first. Other students were spellbound by the stories
of imaginary voyages concocted by the *cuates* (pals). Each of
the Cachuchas grew up to become prominent in the
intellectual, artistic, and political circles of Mexico.

The National Preparatory School offered Frida challenges
and freedoms that she had never known, and never would have
known if she had followed the traditional feminine paths set by
her mother and sisters. The school was part of the National
University, and its rigorous high school curriculum was the
equivalent of college courses. In traveling the hour's distance
from Coyoacán to the school in the center of Mexico City,
Frida left the sheltered suburb, with its Catholic piety and
gentility, to join the passionate activism of Mexican
intellectuals and revolutionaries as they worked to make
Mexican education reflect the values of Mexico, rather than
those of Europe, and to change Mexico from a largely illiterate
society into one in which everybody had access to education.

As one of only thirty-five girls in a student population of
more than two thousand students, Frida chose a course of
study that would lead to medical school. She quickly shed her
proper European schoolgirl clothes and adopted blue overalls.
Her wit and courage endeared her to her male *cuates*, and she
reveled in shocking the proper young ladies. Her female
friends tended to be tomboys or eccentrics, as she was. One of
her favorite places was the Zócala, Mexico's central plaza,
where she associated with Arab newsboys and acquired a rich
vocabulary of obscenities that she never hesitated to use to
good effect.

While she was at school, family financial circumstances
forced Frida to find a job to help pay for her school expenses.
After a few false starts in clerical jobs, at which she was
hopeless, her father found her a job with Fernando Fernández,

a printer. He quickly discovered that his young employee had a talent for drawing, which he put to good use by having her copy prints for engraving.

Frida enjoyed the work and appreciated the opportunities it offered her as an excuse for meeting Alejandro. She had kept their relationship a secret from her family, except Cristina, who sometimes acted as go-between for Frida and her boyfriend. Frida and Alejandro dreamed of going to the United States, and Frida thought that she might be able to save some of her wages toward the trip. Then suddenly, on a rainy September day in 1925, her dreams of medical school and travel with Alejandro were shattered.

Chapter 4

Accidents

Frida and Alejandro decided to ride the bus back to Coyoacán on the afternoon of September 17, 1925. Frida had been shopping and had bought a small parasol and a *balero* (a toy filled with candy). When she found her parasol missing, Frida and her boyfriend got off the first bus they had boarded to look for it. They reboarded another bus, driven by a bus driver whom Frida later described as young and nervous. In front of the San Juan market, a trolley was headed straight for the bus; both vehicles were moving slowly but steadily toward each other. As the trolley rounded the corner, it squeezed the bus into the wall: The bus stretched and stretched until finally it shattered into thousands of pieces. The trolley continued to move, running over some of the passengers.

Alejandro, badly bruised but with no broken bones or severe cuts, pulled himself out from under the trolley and went to look for Frida. He found her totally naked—the force of the accident had torn off all her clothes—and her bloody body was covered in gold dust, probably spilled from a painter's supplies. Bystanders, thinking she was a dancer, shouted, "*La bailarina, la bailarina!*" When he picked her up, he discovered that her body had been pierced by an iron handrail torn from the trolley.

A man who was standing nearby insisted that the rail be pulled from Frida's body. She was still conscious, and her screams of pain sounded louder to Alejandro than the sirens of the Red Cross ambulance that picked her up and rushed her to the hospital. The doctors at the Red Cross Hospital nearly gave Frida up for dead: It was only at the insistence of Alejandro that they decided to operate on her.

The handrail had pierced through her body, entering on the left side at her abdomen and coming out through the pelvic area. There were three breaks in her pelvis, three in her spine, and eleven in her left leg. Her collarbone was broken, as were two ribs. Her left shoulder was dislocated and her right foot was crushed.

The doctors did not know if she would survive, much less walk again. When she regained consciousness, she asked for her family—but her parents had been so shocked by the accident that they were helpless. Only Frida's older sister Matita, who had read about the accident in the newspaper, rushed to her side.

Pain and *La Pelona*

Matita came to the hospital every day to help care for Frida and to cheer her up. Matita's help was badly needed, for Frida was in a ward with twenty-five other patients tended by only one nurse. For a month in the hospital, Frida's body was immobilized in a plaster cast placed within a coffin-like box. The Cachuchas and other friends from school were faithful visitors during the day, but at night, when the ward was dark and quiet, *La Pelona* danced around Frida's bed.

La Pelona, which means the bald, stupid woman, is the name that Frida gave to death. Its presence would haunt her for the rest of her life. Although she greeted and dismissed *La Pelona* with laughter and sarcastic humor, Frida's suffering and the realization of her own fragility tempered her zest for life, her *alegría*. The eighteen-year-old carefree girl suddenly became a woman.

To nearly everyone who came to visit, Frida appeared bright and funny, but in the letters she wrote to Alejandro, she poured out her fears that she would never again be the same person. Yet rather than plunging into despair, she turned to endurance: *No hay remedio*—there is no remedy. "One must put up with it," she wrote. "I am beginning to grow accustomed to suffering."[12]

Frida seemed to recover quickly. She left the hospital after a month and was walking the next month; by mid-December, she was able to travel to Mexico City, and she started working for her father in January, 1926. She was unable to return to school because she had missed her final exams, and her family needed money to help pay her radical expenses.

In the summer of 1926, she had a relapse. A surgeon found that three of the vertebrae in her spine were displaced, and she once more was confined to plaster corsets and not allowed to move. It was during this period of recovery that Frida Kahlo began to paint. Bored, she persuaded her father to lend her his oil paints, and her mother hired a carpenter to construct a kind of easel that she could use while lying in bed. Her first subjects were those that were close at hand: her family, her friends, and herself.

Pain Becomes Art

She painted her first self-portrait as a gift for Alejandro. Their relationship had begun to fall apart, probably because of the strains of separation caused by the aftermath of the accident and by Alejandro's jealousy about her flirtatious behavior. The breakup was difficult for Frida, for she had little else to occupy her.

The self-portrait was meant to beckon Alejandro back to her; it shows the Italian Renaissance influence of Botticelli's classic beauties and the modern elongated effects of Modigliani's women. What resulted was a subdued, gentle, feminine representation of herself dressed in a wine-red velvet dress with a plunging neckline. Her trademark joined eyebrows formed the only slightly jarring feature. Frida was trying to cast herself into the model of a woman who she thought would please Alejandro. They did reconcile for a time, but Alejandro's parents sent him off to Europe in 1927. By the time he returned, the lives of the two young people had begun to go their separate ways, although they would always remain friends.

The idea of painting as a career had begun to tantalize Kahlo. She pored over art books in her father's library and those lent to her by friends. The Cachuchas, who were now embarked on university studies, were immersed in student and national politics. She included herself among them in an early

Frida (left), in a man's suit, only a few months after the accident that nearly killed her. Members of her family include (top row, left to right) her grandmother, sister Adriana, and Adriana's husband; (middle row) an uncle, her mother, and a cousin; (front) nephew Carlos and sister Cristina. (Cenidap Archive)

Cubist-influenced painting entitled *Las Cachuchas*. It depicts a group of sophisticated and highly intense young people. Four of them, including Frida, stare out at the viewers, challenging their perceptions. They were challenging the government and the university administration as well, concerned about two major issues: José Vasconcelos' presidential campaign and the struggle to remove the university from the government's control. Many of the student leaders were also interested in the efforts of the Mexican Communist Party to improve the lot of the peasants and laborers.

Art and Politics

Although Frida was not attending the university, she continued her contacts with her old friends and made new friends among the artistic circles of Mexico City. She met Tina Modotti, an American photographer, through a mutual friend. Tina was a few years older than Frida, and because she was as beautiful as she was talented, she was at the center of the bohemian artistic circle. She and Frida became close friends, and through Tina's influence Frida joined the Young Communist League. Throughout her life, Frida remained an ardent but nondoctrinaire Communist. She strongly believed in the efforts of the Communists to change the Mexican social system, but she never felt obligated to follow the strict dictates of the Party.

It was at a wild party at Tina's house that Frida once again met Diego Rivera, Mexico's most famous muralist. His usual costume was a Stetson hat, baggy overalls, miner's shoes, and a revolver. That night at the party, Diego pulled out his revolver and shot Tina's phonograph. The forty-one-year-old painter had recently returned from Russia and had just divorced Lupe Marín. His ugly charm and fame attracted all sorts of women, who wanted to bask in the great artist's glow. Frida chose a bold approach to get the painter's attention.

She took three of her paintings to the Ministry of Education building, where Rivera was painting a mural. He was standing on a high scaffold when Frida shouted to him, "Diego, please come down from there! I have something important to discuss with you!" When the artist climbed down, she asked him to look at her work and give her his honest opinion on whether she should continue to paint:

> I have to work to earn my livelihood. I have done some paintings which I want you to look over professionally. I want an absolutely straightforward opinion, because I cannot afford to go on just to appease my vanity. I want you to tell me whether you think I can become a good enough artist to make it worth my while to go on.[13]

Rivera looked at them, one by one, and he was immediately impressed. He believed that the canvases revealed an unusual energy of expression, precise delineation of character, true honesty, and an artistic personality of their own. It was obvious to him that this girl was an authentic artist. He told Frida that no matter how difficult it was for her, she must continue to paint.

Frida invited her mentor to Coyoacán the following Sunday to see the rest of her work. When he arrived, Frida was perched in a tree whistling the "Internationale" (the anthem of the Communist revolution). She showed him the rest of her work, and Diego was enchanted: "I did not know it then, but Frida had already become the most important fact in my life."[14]

The years 1925-1928 shaped the rest of Frida Kahlo's life. She grew from a child to a woman and from a student to an artist. Much later she was to say, "I suffered two grave accidents in my life. One in which a streetcar knocked me down . . . The other accident is Diego."[15]

Chapter 5

Sacred Monsters

Rivera followed the first Sunday afternoon visit to Coyoacán with many others; Sunday was the day he quit painting early. When he started to court Frida in earnest, he persuaded her to pose as a young revolutionary in one of his murals, *The Ballad of the Proletarian Revolution*, at the Ministry of Education. One day as he was painting her, he declared to her that she had a dog-face. She immediately retorted that he had the face of a frog. *Carasapo* (frog-face) quickly became her favorite nickname for the great painter, although she continued to call him *Panzón* (fat-belly) and *Dieguito* (little Diego) as well.

Courtship

Diego's relationship with Frida was different from any he had ever had with other women. This young woman was beautiful and passionate, but she was also motherly toward him. Not only did he admire and encourage Frida's painting, but he also respected her opinions concerning his work. Rivera's biographer states that Frida was the only person, male or female, whom he consulted during his mature years about his own work. During their marriage, Diego became more and more interested in his wife's approval and depended on her insightful artistic judgment. For her part, Frida treated Diego as she had treated her old *cuates*; he became her *cuatacho*, her "big pal."

After a few Sunday afternoon visits to Coyoacán, Rivera was approached by Frida's father:

"I see you are interested in my daughter?"

"Why, yes," stammered Diego, anticipating something not altogether agreeable. "Yes, of course, otherwise I would not come all the way out here to see her."

"Well, sir, I want to give you a warning. Frida is a clever girl, but she is *un demonio occulto*—a concealed devil. *Un demonio occulto!*" He solemnly repeated the epithet a second time, with still greater emphasis.

"I know it," replied Diego.

"Well, I have done my duty." The old man said no more.[16]

During the period in which Rivera was courting Kahlo, she began to paint even more seriously. She sought out Rivera's advice, but he was careful not to turn her into his disciple. He sensed that she had her own particular vision, which she had to discover for herself. Kahlo, however, soaked in the atmosphere of the older painter—she watched him paint and she discussed art and politics with him.

The most obvious influences of Rivera's work on Kahlo's style are the changes in her color choices and in her subjects. Kahlo's early paintings had drawn from the somber but rich palettes of European artists. During the period 1928-1929, she turned to the bright and festive colors of Mexico's landscape, its popular art and daily life. Similarly, she took as models Mexican Indian women and children; her treatment of them was straightforward and unsentimental, focusing on the individuality of each subject.

In *The Bus*, a painting from this period, Kahlo's humorous view of the world merges with her growing social consciousness. The painting depicts members of various classes of Mexican society lined up together on the bench of a public bus. At the center of the bench is a barefoot Indian mother suckling one child while her little boy peers out the window at the passing scenery. She is flanked on one side by a harried Mestizo (half Indian, half European) housewife and an

In 1929, Frida and Diego marched in a demonstration of the Syndicate of Technical Workers, Painters, and Sculptors. (Cenidap Archive)

African-Mexican laborer dressed in overalls and holding a wrench. On the other side sit an Anglo-looking man holding a bag of money (he resembles the American silent-film comedian Buster Keaton) and a very modern young woman who resembles Frida's sister Cristina. The bus was the one place where all segments of Mexican society came together. Kahlo credited Rivera in an interview given to a *Time* magazine reporter in 1950: "Diego showed me the revolutionary sense of life and the true sense of color."

The *Self-Portrait* she painted in 1929, the year she married Diego, depicts a very different conception of herself from the one that she had presented three years earlier to Alejandro Gómez. This self-confident young woman beckons no one, except perhaps through the directness of her gaze. She wears a simple white peasant blouse and Mayan jade beads. Next to her on a column is a clock ticking in her ear, and above her head is an airplane flying into the heights of the sky. The two images may represent Frida's desire for new opportunities coupled with her knowledge that even at this young age, the passage of time could close off some of those opportunities. Yet she seems entirely self-possessed and ready to face her future.

Marriage

On August 21, 1929, Frida Kahlo and Diego Rivera were married in a simple civil ceremony in the town hall of Coyoacán. Frida's mother did not attend the ceremony; perhaps she did not approve of her daughter's marrying a Communist atheist who was twice her age. Guillermo Kahlo had given the couple his blessing; undoubtedly he was relieved that his daughter's past and future medical bills would be taken care of. Indeed, Rivera took care of the whole Kahlo family, paying off the mortgage on the Coyoacán house and helping with expenses.

Frida had borrowed her wedding clothes from one of the maids in the household: peasant skirts and blouse and a *rebozo* (a Mexican shawl). Their wedding photograph shows a slender Frida, seated; next to her stands Diego, enormous in a somewhat ill-fitting suit with his sombrero in his hand. Kahlo's parents characterized the union as "the marriage between an elephant and a dove."

Two years after their marriage, Kahlo painted a wedding portrait entitled *Frida and Diego Rivera*. The couple stands stiffly staring outward at the viewer, their hands only lightly clasped. Even at this early stage of their marriage, Frida knew that Diego could not abide possessiveness. Her other hand clasps her *rebozo* around her, in an almost self-protective gesture. Diego stands solidly with his paint palette in his hand; Frida looks tiny beside him, inclining her head toward her husband. It seems she sees him as the great artist, herself as his adoring wife—until one reads the painting's inscription: "Here you see us, me Frieda Kahlo, with my beloved husband Diego Rivera. I painted these portraits in the beautiful city of San Francisco California for our friend Mr. Albert Bender, and it was in the month of April of the year 1931."[17] Here Frida claims for herself the same role she has given to Diego in the portrait. In this painterly inscription, Frida used the German spelling of her name, which she would change to "Frida" when the Nazis rose to power.

It would be a stormy marriage, but a strong partnership was forged that day. Rivera was notorious for his womanizing, and it resumed not long after he had married Kahlo. Among the most prominent of his conquests were the movie stars Paulette Goddard, María Félix, and Dolores del Rio, but most hurtful to Kahlo was the affair with her sister Cristina. Kahlo responded with affairs of her own, most of which she kept secret from Rivera, for he was capable of violent jealousy. Her attachments included the sculptor Isamu Noguchi, New York photographer Nickolas Muray, and Russian revolutionary Leon Trotsky, who had been exiled after conflicts with Soviet dictator Joseph Stalin and found asylum in the Riveras' household. Their friends described Frida and Diego as "sacred monsters," for although they violated all social conventions, they continued to love each other and to create artistic masterpieces.

Partnership

Frida responded in a variety of ways to Diego's affairs, from being deeply hurt to simply dismissing them offhandedly. She once said, "Being the wife of Diego is the most marvelous thing in the world. . . . I let him play matrimony with other women. Diego is not anybody's husband and never will be, but

August, 1929: Frida and Diego Rivera on their wedding day. (Cenidap Archive)

he is a great comrade."[18] Often she became good friends with the women with whom Diego had had or was having relationships.

One interesting example is Lupe Marín, Diego's previous wife. One day shortly after Frida and Diego were married, Lupe came to visit Frida. She looked around the house and immediately took Frida out to buy pots and pans. Then she taught her how to cook Diego's favorite foods. It was Lupe's example that Frida followed when she started to pack Diego a lunch and take it to him on the scaffolding where he worked. Diego's first love, always, was his art. He worked obsessively long hours; he had even been injured by falling off his scaffold because he had fallen asleep while painting. If Frida wanted to spend much time with her husband, she had to accompany him to his painting sites.

It was respect and admiration for each other's skills and vision that ultimately held Kahlo and Rivera together. Their partnership survived mutual infidelities, illnesses, political upheavals, boredom, divorce, and remarriage. Kahlo and Rivera needed each other: She needed his physical and paternal support; he needed her organizational abilities and motherly nurturing. He offered her a wide imaginative vision of the world, and she gave him an insight into the interior workings of the psyche. Frida often painted Diego with a third eye in the center of his forehead—the eye of imagination. She painted herself with Diego in the middle of her own forehead—he was always in her thoughts. Diego revealed her importance to him in his autobiography, when he stated that Frida was "the most important fact in my life."[19]

Chapter 6

Frida in the United States

Shortly after their marriage, Diego faced serious political troubles in Mexico: His Communist views made him a target of conservative officials in the government who were not above shooting their enemies, and his acceptance of mural commissions from governmental agencies and the U.S. Ambassador placed him in disfavor with the Communist Party, which expelled him from its membership in September, 1929. The Riveras chose to seek safety in the United States and in 1930 went to San Francisco, where Diego had commissions from the San Francisco Stock Exchange Luncheon Club and the California School of Fine Arts to paint murals.

They spent the better part of the next three years in San Francisco, Detroit, and New York, where Diego was praised as a great artist and criticized for his revolutionary Communist themes. The Riveras moved in the most fashionable social circles: business tycoons such as the Fords, the Rockefellers, and the Goodyears, as well as the elite of the intellectual and artistic worlds. All the while, Diego was painting the walls of American institutions with his vision of a world of industrial workers and revolution against capitalist exploitation. It was a situation full of irony, black humor, and finally disaster.

San Francisco

Controversy surrounded the arrival of Diego Rivera in San Francisco because the art community, while it generally acknowledged Rivera's skill as a painter, was dismayed that he, a Mexican communist, should be commissioned by the Stock Exchange, a cornerstone of the American capitalist

Self Portrait (1948): *Frida Kahlo often favored the costume of the Indian women of the Tehuantepec isthmus. In Tehuantepec culture, the women control the economic and political life. Kahlo was familiar with the customs of the Tehuana from Diego Rivera's travels to the isthmus and from Tina Modotti's photographs of Tehuanas gracefully balancing baskets of laundry and fruits on their heads. The wedding costume of the Tehuana, in which Kahlo painted herself twice, consists of a white lace* huipil, *a headdress with openings for the face and arms. The Tehuantepecs created the headdress from a petticoat found in a trunk washed ashore from a shipwreck—they thought it should be worn on the head.* (Reproduction authorized by National Institute of Fine Arts and Literature, Mexico City)

system. However, the geniality of the great painter and the exotic charm of his wife soon won over most of his critics.

Frida had adopted the traditional dress of the Mexican peasant woman, most often that of the Tehuantepec isthmus: an embroidered blouse with a long purple or red skirt over ruffled petticoats. The costume served multiple purposes for Frida. Practically, it allowed her to hide her deformed leg, and it pleased Diego. More important, the costume allowed her to identify with the people and culture of Mexico.

Frida had always recognized the importance of clothes in the creation of her individual persona. As a student she had shed European schoolgirl clothes for the overalls and jeans that proclaimed her solidarity with her *cuates* and the working people of Mexico. Photographs taken of her by her father show her in a variety of costumes, from a man's suit to a velvet dress—costumes that reflect her "trying on" of different roles. Yet the Tehuana costume, accompanied by exotic jewelry and elaborate arrangements of ribbons and flowers in her hair, became the trademark of her strikingly individual style. Sometimes she even painted her costume as a substitute for herself—although it usually then signifies a lonely absence.

Photographs of Frida taken by the famous photographers Edward Weston and Imogen Cunningham during the sojourn in San Francisco show her with heavy Mexican jewelry and her *rebozo* wrapped around her in the fashion adopted by *soldaderas* (the women who accompanied and fought alongside Mexican revolutionaries). Later, when she walked the streets in New York, a young boy followed her, asking, "Where's the circus?" Although Frida came to the United States as Mrs. Diego Rivera, she did not fade away behind his magnetic presence; she quickly became a personality in her own right. One advantage she had over Diego was that she spoke more English than he did.

Kahlo painted a number of portraits of friends and

acquaintances while Rivera was feverishly working at his murals. One was of Dr. Leo Eloesser, a prominent surgeon whom Kahlo consulted in San Francisco and with whom she became close friends. He was to remain her most trusted medical adviser for the rest of her life. His portrait borrowed from the style of nineteenth-century Mexican portraiture, unlike the more fashionable portraits she painted of her acquaintances among the San Francisco elite.

By far the most interesting portrait Kahlo painted while she was in San Francisco was *Luther Burbank*. This portrait of the recently deceased horticulturist, considered the father of the crossbreeding of plants, is the first painting by Kahlo to move away from realism. Here Luther Burbank "grows" from a tree trunk whose roots are being nourished from his own corpse. Two trees, one fully grown with small fruits and another small one with large fruits, probably indicate the results of Burbank's experiments. The connection between life and death, which became a prominent theme in Kahlo's paintings, is here displayed for the first time. The fantastic quality of Kahlo's representation is startling, but absolutely true to the essence of Burbank's life and work.

Frida was fascinated with some aspects of American culture, particularly those that revealed America's diversity. She fell in love with San Francisco's Chinatown and was enchanted by the beauty of Chinese children. However, she was much less enchanted with the hollowness of upper-class cultural customs—cocktail parties and high society functions— especially in the face of the misery that the Great Depression was causing so many Americans. Despite Diego's fascination for the technological wonders of the United States—the country's growing highway system, its fantastic bridges, and its ingenious factories—Frida found most of the industrial advances both impersonal and ugly. She came to see the United States as a threatening *Gringolandia* (land of

Eating ice cream, with Diego on Long Island, New York, in 1933. (Cenidap Archive)

foreigners), which was slowly creeping into her beloved
Mexico.

Detroit

Rivera was commissioned by the Detroit Arts Commission,
headed by Edsel Ford, to paint murals in the Garden Court of
the Detroit Institute of Arts on the theme of modern industry,
particularly that of Detroit, home of the automobile industry.
Rivera was delighted with the commission and the opportunity
to plunge into the factories and the lives of the workers. In his
autobiography he expressed his excitement: "I now placed the
collective hero, man-and-machine, higher than the old
traditional heroes of art and legend."[20]

Although Frida was pleased that Diego was happy with his
work, her time in Detroit was much less pleasant. She found

1. *Self-Portrait*, 1926. (Reproduction authorized by National Institute of Fine Arts and Literature, Mexico City)

2. *The Bus*, 1929. (Reproduction authorized by National Institute of Fine Arts and Literature, Mexico City)

3. *Self-Portrait*, 1929. (Reproduction authorized by National Institute of Fine Arts and Literature, Mexico City)

4. *Frida and Diego Rivera*, 1931. (Reproduction authorized by National Institute of Fine Arts and Literature, Mexico City)

5. *Luther Burbank*, 1931. (Reproduction authorized by National Institute of Fine Arts and Literature, Mexico City)

5. *Henry Ford Hospital*, 1932. (Reproduction authorized by National Institute of Fine Arts and Literature, Mexico City)

7. *Self-Portrait on the Border Line Between Mexico and the United States*, 1932.
(Reproduction authorized by National Institute of Fine Arts and Literature, Mexico City)

8. *My Dress Hangs There*, 1933. (Reproduction authorized by National Institute of Fine Arts and Literature, Mexico City)

9. *What the Water Gave Me*, 1938. (Reproduction authorized by National Institute of Fine Arts and Literature, Mexico City)

10. *Self-Portrait, Dedicated to Leon Trotsky,* 1937. (Reproduction authorized by National Institute of Fine Arts and Literature, Mexico City)

11. *My Grandparents, My Parents, and I*, 1936. (Reproduction authorized by National Institute of Fine Arts and Literature, M＜ City)

12. *The Suicide of Dorothy Hale*, 1939. (Reproduction authorized by National Institute of Fine Arts and Literature, Mexico City)

13. *My Nurse and I*, 1937. (Reproduction authorized by National Institute of Fine Arts and Literature, Mexico City)

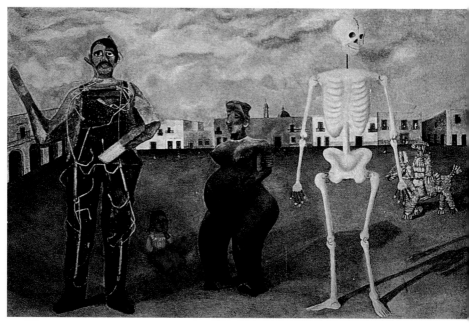

14. *Four Inhabitants of Mexico*, 1938. (Reproduction authorized by National Institute of Fine Arts and Literature, Mexico City)

the city shabby and ugly, and the society in Detroit was much
more snobbish and bigoted than that of San Francisco or New
York. Both Diego and Frida had occasion to flaunt their
Jewish heritage when faced with anti-Semitism. They had
rented an apartment across the street from the Institute of Arts
in a large residential hotel called the Wardell. When Diego
discovered that the hotel had a policy of not renting to Jews, he
declared to the management that he and Frida would have to
leave, since both had Jewish blood. The management, anxious
to keep their famous customers, insisted that the policy did not
include the Riveras and offered to lower their rent. Diego
refused to remain unless the hotel changed its policy, which it
did. Later, at a dinner party hosted by Henry Ford, who was an
avowed anti-Semite, Frida, during a lull in the conversation,
turned to the automobile magnate and "innocently" asked him,
"Mr. Ford, are you Jewish?"

Frida's boredom turned to tragedy on July 4, 1932, when
she hemorrhaged and suffered a miscarriage. The old damage
to her pelvis would not allow her to carry a child to term. She
spent thirteen days in Henry Ford Hospital crying and
bleeding. At one point she asked the doctors to give her some
medical books so she could imagine what her dead fetus had
looked like. When they refused, thinking it was a morbid
request, Diego managed to find a preserved fetus and brought
it to Frida, knowing that she needed to transform her pain into
art. What resulted was a series of drawings and paintings that
vividly and graphically depicted the agony she suffered during
the miscarriage.

Perhaps the most significant is a painting entitled *Henry
Ford Hospital*. Following the *ex-voto* tradition, Kahlo painted
her misfortune on a small metal sheet. However, she departed
radically from the space and devotional theme of the *ex-voto*.
The hospital bed, on which a distorted and bleeding Frida lies,
is set in a no-man's-land with factories rising on the horizon.

Around her bed float six objects which embody the confused emotions Kahlo faced during her ordeal. Above the bed, in the center, is the lost male fetus; to its left is a medical model of what the female torso, including the reproductive organs, should look like; to its right is a snail, which symbolized for Kahlo the process of the miscarriage—slow, soft, covered with a hard shell, yet open and vulnerable. Below the bed are her own broken pelvis, responsible for the miscarriage; a large lavender orchid, which Diego had brought to her in the hospital; and a machine that represented the mechanical aspect of her stay in the hospital. In this *ex-voto* there is no divine intervention to save Frida from disaster; the agent of salvation is modern medicine, and the saved victim has mixed feelings about her rescue. *Henry Ford Hospital* is a radical departure from Kahlo's earlier work, a development noted by Rivera:

> Frida began to work on a series of masterpieces which had no precedent in the history of art—paintings which exalted the feminine qualities of endurance of truth, reality, cruelty, and suffering. Never before had a woman put such agonized poetry on canvas as Frida did at this time in Detroit.[21]

Kahlo's growing distaste for the United States and her longing to return to Mexico are shown in two works, *Self-Portrait on the Border Line Between Mexico and the United States*, painted in Detroit in 1932, and *My Dress Hangs There*, painted the next year in New York. In *Self-Portrait*, Kahlo paints herself standing on a pedestal in a very proper pink evening gown, with a cigarette in one hand and the Mexican flag in the other; the pedestal straddles the border between Mexico and the United States. On the Mexican side the roots of tropical plants dig deep into the ground, which is littered with pre-Columbian statues and a ruined Aztec temple. The cords of electrical appliances reach into the ground of the United States, one plugged into the pedestal on which Frida stands. Here nothing grows but machines, factories, and windowless skyscrapers. The smokestacks of a Ford factory spew smoke into the sky and engulf an image of the American flag. In contrast, the clouds above Mexico contain both the sun and the moon, meeting in a clash of lightning. The dual image of sun and moon is borrowed from Aztec imagery and appears often in Kahlo's later works.

New York City

Frida's empty dress hangs among a Cubist collage representation of her impressions of New York in *My Dress Hangs There*. The dress hangs from a blue ribbon held aloft between two columns displaying representations of two American obsessions: sports (represented by a golf trophy) and plumbing (represented by a toilet). New York landmarks are overlaid with symbols of monetary value. Trinity Church displays a dollar sign in its stained-glass window, and the steps of Federal Hall are made up of a stock market graph. Mae West, the American sex goddess of the day, poses in a huge billboard on the left, and on the right appears a garbage can filled with the castoffs of a consumer society. The foreground of the painting is filled with tiny images of people crowded together and dwarfed by skyscrapers and factories. In the background New York harbor beckons with a steamship that might carry Frida back to Mexico.

The Riveras were in New York because Diego had been commissioned by business magnate (and later Vice President) Nelson Rockefeller to paint a mural in the RCA Building amidst Rockefeller Center, the heart of the banking district in New York. Again the situation was full of contradictions. John D. Rockefeller, Jr. (Nelson's father and the founder of the business empire based on Standard Oil) was footing the bill for a mural with strongly socialist content. The theme of the painting was "Men at the Crossroads Looking with Hope and

High Vision to the Choosing of a New and Better Future."
Rivera's design was divided into two contrasting images. On
one side, Wall Street businessmen binged on food and drink
while unemployed workers and protestors were bullied by the
police. The alternative vision, on the other side, was a Marxist
utopia in which workers, soldiers, families, athletes, and
teachers worked together to build a better world.

At first tickets were sold to watch Rivera work, and the
public made it one of the liveliest shows in town. As Diego
worked feverishly fourteen or fifteen hours a day, Frida took in
the pleasures of Manhattan. She loved department stores, dime

New York, 1933 (left to right): Friend and assistant Lucienne Bloch with Diego and
Frida at the New Worker's School. (Cenidap Archive)

stores, drug stores, Chinatown, and most of all the movies—especially Tarzan films, which she found hysterically funny. She also had many friends in New York who shared her artistic interests and sensibilities. Soon, however, the acclaim gave way to notoriety.

As Rivera's design emerged, the press wrote sensationalistic reports about its Marxist content. The crowds at Rockefeller Center grew hostile and were soon banned from the premises. The capitalists who had supported the mural became nervous. When Rivera included a portrait of Communist leader Vladimir Ilich Lenin in the mural, Nelson Rockefeller wrote a letter asking Rivera to remove it. Rivera refused, and the work at Rockefeller Center was halted. A huge controversy arose with demonstrations and counter-demonstrations. Rivera's work was defended by union workers, artists, and intellectuals.

Frida, too, was active in the campaign to save her husband's work, but to no avail: The Rockefellers reclaimed the wall and removed the mural. Fortunately, one of the Riveras' friends had smuggled in a camera to photograph the mural, and Rivera used her pictures to reconstruct the mural in Mexico City's Palace of Fine Arts in 1934. However, the blow was devastating to Diego, and he was finally persuaded— somewhat against his will—to leave New York. Frida and Diego set sail for Mexico on December 20, 1933.

Chapter 7

Life in Mexico

It was a strange sight: the aging and weary Russian revolutionary with his retiring wife, being led down the gangplank by a flamboyant Mexican woman. Leon Trotsky had just arrived in Mexico seeking asylum from persecution by Joseph Stalin, the ruthless leader of the Soviet Union, who disagreed with Trotsky's vision of a Communist world order. Trotsky and his wife, Natalia, had spent nine years in exile, traveling from country to country. Each time they had settled somewhere, the Stalinist government had put pressure on that country's government to force Trotsky to leave. At the end of 1936, when the Trotskys thought they might never find a place to settle, Diego Rivera went to President Lázaro Cárdenas and secured his permission for Trotsky to come to Mexico.

A Home for Exiles

The Riveras had taken great care to ensure the Trotskys' safety when they arrived in Mexico. Friends of the Trotskys met the boat when it arrived in Tampico on January 9, 1937. Frida represented Diego because he was in the hospital at the time. President Cárdenas had arranged for a special train to transport the exiles from Tampico to Mexico City. The Riveras offered the house in Coyoacán as residence for the Trotskys, and they lived there for two years rent-free. The front windows had been filled in with adobe bricks, and members of the Trotsky faction of the Communist Party helped to stand guard at the house. Frida would serve as the Trotskys' chauffeur, and she made sure the servants hired to help them were entirely trustworthy. Diego even went so far as to buy the house next door when it became apparent that the Riveras' house might be attacked from that direction.

At first the two couples saw much of each other: They often ate dinner together, and the Riveras would take the Trotskys on excursions outside Mexico City and into the mountains. However, the couples could not have been more dissimilar. Leon Trotsky was formal, very methodical, and steadfast— even rigid—in his beliefs concerning how best to reform the world. Diego was expansive and friendly, hated schedules, and often indulged his tendency to exaggerate and fantasize. Natalia Trotsky was warm but tended to fade behind her famous husband. At fifty-five, careworn and tired, she was no rival for the beauty and vitality of her twenty-nine-year-old hostess.

Flattered by Leon Trotsky's obvious admiration, Frida was attracted by his intelligence and imposing presence. She was also intrigued by the prospect of getting back at Diego for his affair with her sister. To have an affair with his friend would be nearly as outrageous. Trotsky and Kahlo thus entered into a brief liaison in the summer of 1937, and luckily Diego did not know of it at the time.

As time went on, the Trotskys and Riveras drifted apart both socially and politically. Neither Frida nor Diego could long be restrained by any rigid political philosophy, and Trotsky's dogmatism became less attractive. Eventually the discord between Trotsky and Rivera grew to such an extent that the Trotskys moved out of the house in Coyoacán.

A Home for Intellectuals

During this time, Frida had been actively involved in relief efforts for the victims of the Spanish Civil War (1936-1939). She was an ardent supporter of the Spanish Republicans in their ultimately futile attempts to halt the rise of Fascist forces led by General Francisco Franco. She welcomed into her home

An intellectual circle, 1938 (left to right): Leon Trotsky, Diego Rivera, Natalia Trotsky, Reba Hansen, André Breton, Frida, and Jean Van Heijenoort (Trotsky's secretary). (Cenidap Archive)

Spanish soldiers who had come to seek economic aid for the Republican Loyalist forces, and she worked to raise funds for their struggle.

The Riveras' house was a gathering place for the international artistic and intellectual community that came to Mexico City. When the Riveras had returned from New York, they had moved into a residence designed for them in San Ángel. The house—two cubes linked by a bridge—reflected the marriage of Rivera and Kahlo, two strong personalities linked by their love for each other. Rivera's pink cube, the larger of the two, contained a high-ceilinged, semi-public studio, where guests were entertained, and a large kitchen in which most meals were eaten; like Diego, it was an open, outgoing space. Kahlo's blue cube was a more traditional home, with a ground-level garage, a living area and kitchen on the floor above it, and a bedroom/studio on the third floor; like Frida, her cube was more private and personal.

Kahlo's studio was increasingly in use as she turned thirty. The years 1937 and 1938 were her most productive thus far in numbers of paintings. She was relatively healthy during this time and focused on her work. In 1937 she completed nearly a dozen paintings, and in 1938, she completed more than a dozen. The subjects varied from still-lifes to autobiographical depictions of her childhood, from portraits of her acquaintances and Diego to a bathtub vision entitled *What the Water Gave Me*, and, of course, a number of self-portraits, many of them containing images of the monkeys that now wandered in and out of the Riveras' household. The still-lifes, depicting Mexican fruits and vegetables, were symbolic of the connections between life and death in the natural cycle. All the paintings from this period are strongly grounded in Kahlo's Mexican consciousness, and they often include fantastic and dream-like images. Her style became more confident and her techniques more accomplished.

As Frida painted more, Diego encouraged her to exhibit and sell her paintings. He arranged for the first major sale of her paintings to American film star Edward G. Robinson, who was a noted art collector. He and his wife had come to Rivera's studio, and as Frida chatted with Mrs. Robinson on the terrace, Diego took Robinson into Frida's studio and showed him her paintings. Robinson bought four of Kahlo's paintings at two hundred dollars each. Frida was delighted: Selling her paintings would give her a kind of freedom she had not known before—no longer did she need to depend on Diego for money to travel or to do what she wanted. However, as important as this first major sale was to Frida financially, two other events in 1938 would secure her international reputation.

Painting What the Water Gave Me *in 1938.* (Cenidap Archive)

Chapter 8

Recognition

As a result of Kahlo's inclusion in a group show at the Galería de Arte in September, 1937, she received a letter from Julien Levy, a New York art dealer who specialized in Surrealist art. Someone had recommended her paintings to Levy. When she sent him photographs of her work, he was very excited and offered her a solo show at his gallery.

Surrealism

During the time she was completing work for Levy, André Breton, poet and leader of the French Surrealist movement, came to Mexico to discover new forms of Surrealistic expression. Surrealism was an artistic and literary movement founded in Paris in 1924 by Breton with the publication of his *Surrealist Manifesto*. Surrealism emphasized the role of the unconscious and dream imagery in creative activity. As an organized movement, it remained under the leadership of Breton, but many artists—including Salvador Dalí, Pablo Picasso, Joan Miró, and Frida Kahlo—would, both intentionally and unintentionally, use Surrealist techniques and ideas in their works.

Like other intellectuals who visited Mexico, Breton gravitated to the Riveras and engaged in long theoretical conversations with both Diego and Trotsky. Kahlo was utterly bored with their discussions, but Breton was enchanted with her paintings. He saw in her an unconscious Surrealist and wrote an essay for the brochure that accompanied Julien Levy's show. In the brochure he described Frida's work as a "ribbon around a bomb" and went on to exult:

> My surprise and joy were unbounded when I discovered, on my
> arrival in Mexico, that her work had blossomed forth, in her latest
> paintings, into pure surreality, despite the fact that it had been
> conceived without any prior knowledge whatsoever of the ideas
> motivating the activities of my friends and myself. . . . I was
> witnessing here, at the other end of the earth, a spontaneous
> outpouring of our own questioning spirit. . . . This art even contains
> that drop of cruelty and humor uniquely capable of blending the rare
> effective powers that compound together to form the philtre which is
> Mexico's secret.[22]

Breton offered Kahlo a one-woman show in Paris after the
exhibition in New York had closed.

The Surrealistic elements that Breton and Levy saw in
Kahlo's work were particularly evident in such paintings as
My Birth, My Nurse and I, Henry Ford Hospital, and *What the
Water Gave Me.* The last, painted in 1938, is perhaps her most
"Surrealistic" painting. In it, Kahlo shows her toes pressing
against the edge of the bathtub. Her wounded right foot is
deformed and bleeding, as is the drain above her toe. In the
water between her knees and toes float the "toys" of Frida's
imagination. The only recognizable people are her parents,
partially hidden behind dense foliage. Below her parents, two
female nudes are perched on a sponge (Kahlo reproduced them
in a larger image in the painting *Two Nudes in a Forest,* which
she completed the next year). The Empire State Building rises
from a volcano on an island which also contains a *calavera*
(skeleton), a dead bird atop a tree, and a sunbather. The
sunbather holds in his hand a rope, which loops first around
the neck of a strangled nude, floating in the water, then around
an outcropping of rocks, and finally back to the island, where
it is anchored around a stone. Along the rope crawl insects and
a worm, surrounding a tiny tightrope walker doing her
balancing act. The bathwater also contains a red flower,
Frida's Tehuana dress, a conch shell spouting water, and a ship
with sails in full billow.

André Breton founded the Surrealist movement in 1924, when he published his Surrealist
Manifesto. *Surrealism influenced both literature and painting. The Surrealists were
interested in liberating the "inner truth" by rebelling against the rational consciousness
of Western thought. In order to tap into the unconscious, Surrealists used dream imagery,
automatic writing, Freudian psychology, and primitive art traditions. The movement
influenced such artists as Giorgio de Chirico, Marc Chagall, Paul Klee, Marcel
Duchamp, Pablo Picasso, and Salvador Dalí.* (AP/Wide World Photos)

The painting is both disturbing and amusing. It contains images of death and fertility, but there is no central image or dominating focus. In *What the Water Gave Me*, Kahlo painted the floating bath of her consciousness.

Shocking Images

What the Water Gave Me was one of twenty-five paintings that Kahlo took with her to New York to exhibit at the Julien Levy Gallery. Diego remained behind in Mexico to work, but he sent with Frida a list of people to invite to the opening on November 1, 1938. On the list were prominent public figures such as Mr. and Mrs. Nelson Rockefeller and politician and diplomat Clare Boothe Luce, as well as artistic friends and acquaintances such as sculptor Isamu Noguchi, photographer and gallery owner Alfred Stieglitz, painter Georgia O'Keeffe, sculptor Louise Nevelson, and photographer Nickolas Muray, with whom Frida was having an affair during her stay in New York.

The press generally was favorable toward Kahlo's work, but the reviews took on a somewhat patronizing tone. The reporter from *Time* magazine declared, "*Little* Frida's pictures, mostly painted in oil on copper, had the daintiness of miniatures, the vivid reds and yellows of Mexican tradition and the playfully bloody fancy of an unsentimental child."[23] Critics were still finding it difficult to take women artists seriously, even if collectors did. More than half of the paintings were sold directly from the exhibition. The show also resulted in commissions for Kahlo.

On the night of the exhibit, Clare Boothe Luce asked Kahlo to paint a memorial work of her friend Dorothy Hale, who had recently committed suicide by jumping from the window of her top-floor suite at the Hampshire House. The *recuerdo* (memorial portrait) that Mrs. Luce received from Kahlo, *The Suicide of Dorothy Hale*, was hardly what she had expected. In the center of the painting a white skyscraper rises behind the clouds of a pale blue sky. Kahlo had painted the act of Hale's suicide in three stages: a tiny figure near the top of the building just having leapt from the window, a midsize figure tumbling headfirst down to the ground, and a prone, bleeding body spread across the bottom of the painting, her foot falling out onto the inscription below. The frame around the picture is an important part of the work, for Kahlo refused to let it enclose the painting: The clouds spread out onto the sides and top of the frame, and Hale's blood drips onto its lower edge. Mrs. Luce was horrified:

> I will always remember the shock I had when I pulled the painting out of the crate. I felt really physically *sick*. What was I going to do with this gruesome painting of the smashed corpse of my dead friend, and her blood dripping down all over the frame. I could not return it—across the top of the painting there was an angel waving an unfurled banner which proclaimed in Spanish that this was "The Suicide of Dorothy Hale, painted at the request of Clare Boothe Luce. . . ." I would not have requested such a gory picture of my worst enemy, much less of my unfortunate friend.[24]

Her first impulse was to destroy the painting, but she allowed a friend to take it away on the condition that someone would paint over the banner proclaiming that she had commissioned the work. Kahlo later included the painting in her Paris show.

Although Frida had enjoyed her stay in New York and was sought out by many admirers, she was suffering from pain in her right foot and an aching spine. In fact, she was seriously ill after her show closed and hesitated to go to Paris, both because of her illness and because she missed Diego. Diego encouraged her to go, however, so she set sail for France in January, 1939.

International Recognition

When Frida reached Paris, everything was in disarray.
Breton had done nothing to arrange a gallery, and her paintings
were still sitting in the customs house. For a while Frida stayed
with the Bretons until she became ill with a kidney infection
and had to be hospitalized. After she recovered, she moved in
with Mary Reynolds, a friend of the painter Marcel Duchamp.
It was Duchamp who finally arranged for her paintings to be
shown at the Galérie Pierre Colle. The exhibit opened on
March 10, 1939, a month and a half later than Frida had
expected.

The show was not a financial success for Kahlo. The threat
of World War II had tightened everyone's pocketbooks, and
French collectors did not welcome a foreign artist, especially a
woman artist. However, her work did receive a favorable
review, and one of her paintings, *The Frame*, was bought by
the Louvre museum and is now in the collection of the
National Museum of Modern Art at the Georges Pompidou
Center. More important was the recognition by the Parisian art
world. Frida wrote on March 17, 1939, in a letter to Ella and
Bertram Wolfe:

> There were a lot of people on the day of the opening, great
> congratulations to the "chicua," amongst them a big hug from Joan
> Miró and great praises for my painting from Kandinsky,
> congratulations from Picasso and Tanguy, from Paalen, and from
> other "big cacas" of Surrealism. In sum I can say that it was a success,
> and taking into account the quality of the taffy (that is to say the
> crowd of congratulators) I believe that the thing went well
> enough. . . .[25]

Frida became acquainted with some of the important figures
in Surrealist circles, such as poet Paul Éluard and painter Max
Ernst, and she frequented artists' cafés and learned to love
American jazz, which was the rage at Parisian nightclubs. The

fashion world also took note of her presence in Paris—her hands, decked with many rings, appeared on the cover of *Vogue*, and the famous designer Giovanni Schiaparelli designed a *robe Madame Rivera* based on Frida's Tehuana costume. Nevertheless, Frida disliked the pretentiousness of French intellectuals. She found their conversation empty and their lives wasted. On February 16, 1939, she wrote to Nickolas Muray:

> . . . those "artistic" bitches of Paris. They sit for hours on the "cafes" warming their precious behinds, and talk without stopping about "culture" "art" "revolution" and so on and so forth, thinking themselves the gods of the world, dreaming their most fantastic nonsenses, and poisoning the air with theories. . . . I never seen Diego or you wasting their time on stupid gossip and "intellectual" discussions, that is why you are real *men* and not lousy "artists."[26]

While Frida was disgusted with the do-nothingness of the Parisian intellectuals, she busied herself with arranging for the emigration of four hundred Spanish Loyalist refugees to Mexico. Finally, on March 25, 1939, she was able to sail from Le Havre, on the north coast of France, back to New York and then on to Mexico.

Her Own Reality

The shows in New York and Paris helped Kahlo achieve recognition of her position as a professional artist. On her return home she was invited to show her work in the "International Exhibition of Surrealism" at the Galería de Arte Mexicano. She sent two works: *The Wounded Table* and *The Two Fridas*. The Mexican government recognized her international status and asked her to curate exhibitions at the Palace of Fine Arts and National Painting Fair. She was also a founding member of the Seminario de Cultura Mexicana, a group of twenty-five artists and intellectuals who were chosen by the government to spread Mexican culture throughout the country with their lectures and exhibitions. During the decade of the 1940's, Kahlo's work was shown in exhibitions in London, Paris, Stockholm, San Francisco, Boston, Philadelphia, and New York. The government of Mexico awarded Kahlo the National Prize of Arts and Sciences in 1946.

Kahlo's reputation was made by her association with the Surrealists, but it was an association with which she was always somewhat uncomfortable. There is no doubt that she was aware of the popularity and influence of the Surrealists in the 1920's and 1930's, and that she was aware of their experimentation with dream-like and fantastic images. Nevertheless, when Breton claimed her as part of the Surrealist camp, she stated:

> I never knew I was a Surrealist till André Breton came to Mexico and told me I was. The only thing I know is that I paint because I need to, and I paint always whatever passes through my head without any other consideration.[27]

Kahlo never subscribed to the theoretical and intellectual statements of the European Surrealist school. The fantastic images that she reproduced in her paintings came directly from her experience as a Mexican and from her own life. The fantastic and macabre have always played an important role in the fiestas and spirit of Mexico. Combined with her cultural heritage, Frida's intense pain, her losses, and her sense of humor created a unique form of Surrealism that emphasized its playful aspects: "I use Surrealism as a means of poking fun at others without their realizing it, and of making friends with those who do realize it."[28] Near the end of her life, she declared her independence: "They thought I was a Surrealist, but I wasn't. I never painted dreams. I painted my own reality."[29]

Chapter 9

Murdered by Life

The new painting instructor, a woman, swept into the offices of La Esmeralda, the Ministry of Education's School of Painting and Sculpture, asking another instructor, "What's this about teaching? I don't know anything about teaching." The other instructor was very angry and asked one of his pupils, "How can she be a teacher if she doesn't know anything about teaching?"

Frida Kahlo may not have known anything about the theoretical or standard practices of teaching, but she had a natural sympathy for her students and was concerned that their art be honest and connected to their own lives. La Esmeralda had been founded in 1942 to prepare its students to express their creativity in the arts. Its doors were open to all; tuition and art materials were free. The distinguished faculty, who at first outnumbered the students, included prominent Mexican artists such as Jesús Guerrero Galván, Carlos Orozco Romero, María Izquierdo, Diego Rivera, and Frida Kahlo. One of Kahlo's students, the painter Fanny Rabel, remembers her first impression of the new instructor.

Fanny was not looking forward to having a woman teacher, because up to that time she had had only male teachers and male companions. Almost everything in Mexico was managed by men, and there were very few girls in the school. Her doubts vanished, however, the moment she met Kahlo; she became fascinated with this woman of enormous *alegría*, humor, and love of life. Frida "invented her own language, her own way of speaking Spanish, full of vitality and accompanied by gestures, mimicry, laughter, jokes, and great sense of irony."[30] The new instructor created an informal relationship with all her students, to whom she became like a big sister, a mother watching her *muchachitos*.

Kahlo dragged her students out in the streets to paint the life of Mexico. They went to convents and slums, to markets and Aztec pyramids. Her aim was to stimulate her pupils and open their eyes to the beauty of the people and the art that they produced. Her enthusiasm struck a chord in her students. She encouraged them to paint in their own way, using only the standard of beauty as the basis for critique. She was not interested in theory, but she did teach her students to be critical of their own efforts.

After a few months of commuting to Mexico City to teach at La Esmeralda, Kahlo's health began to deteriorate, and she could no longer make the long trip. She invited her students to come to Coyoacán to continue their lessons. At first, a large

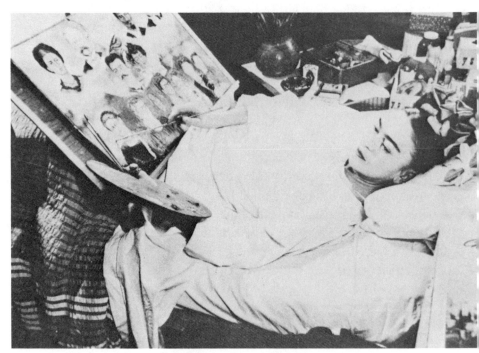

1951: Painting My Family *in a hospital in England.* (Cenidap Archive)

group traveled to Coyoacán, but many of the students found the bus ride too time-consuming and dropped her class. Four students, however, faithfully remained with Frida for years—even after they had graduated from school. Arturo García Bustos, Arturo Estrada, Guillermo Monroy, and Fanny Rabel became known as *Los Fridos*, Frida's special protégés.

She turned the garden of the Coyoacán house over to them and left them to paint there while she worked in her studio. The garden was not only filled with plants, but with the Riveras' menagerie, which included monkeys, parrots, and little itzcuintli dogs. The occasions on which Frida emerged to critique her students' work turned into parties: She served refreshments and sometimes took her students to the movies afterward. Occasionally Diego would join the sessions, adding his comments to Frida's.

Divorce and Remarriage

Frida and Diego had finally settled into a companionable, if sometimes stormy, relationship after they had divorced in 1939 and subsequently remarried on December 8, 1940. Their remarriage took place in San Francisco, where Kahlo had joined Rivera after she had spent two days in jail in Mexico City.

Because Leon Trotsky had been assassinated by a Stalinist revolutionary whom Frida had known, the police suspected she was involved in the assassination attempt. She and her sister Cristina were jailed for two days while the police questioned them about the murder. When she was released, she joined Rivera in San Francisco, where the two were finally reconciled through the advice of Dr. Eloesser. During the period of the divorce, Frida and Diego had rediscovered the basic mutual needs and the support that only they could offer to each other.

Upon their return to Mexico, they moved their major residence out to the house in Coyoacán, which they had painted blue and decorated with Mexican furnishings, because its layout was more convenient for Frida as she became increasingly disabled by her deteriorating spine and foot. Diego kept the house in San Ángel as his studio and city residence.

Los Fridos Paint Murals

Los Fridos also benefitted from the dual influence of Kahlo and Rivera. Knowing that her pupils had studied mural painting with Rivera, Kahlo arranged for them to paint new murals on the outside walls of a local *pulquería* called La Rosita. Kahlo and Rivera oversaw the project, but all the painting was done by students from La Esmeralda.

In 1945, another mural opportunity was offered to Los Fridos. The government had built public laundries equipped with separate rooms for washing, ironing, dining, child-care, and meeting, and the laundry in Coyoacán became a project for Los Fridos. Each of the students created separate designs for the various projects, consulting with the laundresses and with one another. All helped to paint the individual panels with paint and brushes supplied by Kahlo and refreshments supplied by the laundresses. Public officials, teachers, and students were invited to the opening of the laundry, and it provided a showcase for the students.

Throughout the period during which Kahlo taught Los Fridos, she found opportunities to help further their careers. After they finished their studies, they remained her friends and often attributed their success to her guidance.

Declining Health

After 1944, Frida was beset with worsening health. She underwent numerous operations and hospitalizations, and to support her spine she was forced to wear a series of orthopedic corsets, without which she often could neither sit nor stand.

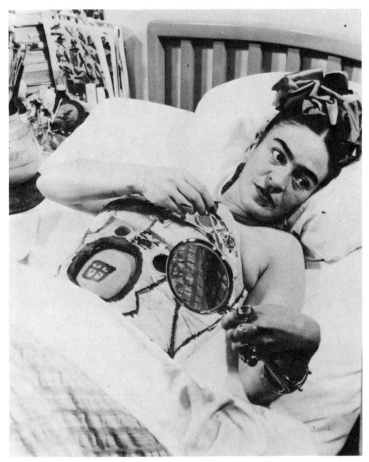

Frida spent an entire year (1950-1951) in an English hospital; here she paints a plaster cast that engulfed her torso. (Cenidap Archive)

Her paintings from this period reflect an obsession with her physical condition and attempts to cope with her pain through her art. Two particularly illuminating works are *The Broken Column* (1944) and *The Little Deer* (1946).

In *The Broken Column*, Kahlo paints herself in full frontal torso. She holds a drape around the lower part of her body, and the upper part is held together by a steel corset. A fissure opens from her chin, down her neck, between her breasts, and into her pelvis. It reveals a cracked and crumbling Ionic column where her spine should be. The fissure down her body

87

echoes the fissures in the *pedregal* landscape behind her. It is as if she realizes that the broken quality of her body reflects, and is intimately connected with, a harshly broken nature. In *The Broken Column*, Kahlo has pierced her flesh with nails and her eyes weep tears, but her expression is stoic, even defiant. She has painted herself with the images of a martyred saint, but she seeks no salvation from her pain—only confrontation and acknowledgment.

In *The Little Deer*, Kahlo sets her head atop a young stag that has been shot with nine arrows. The expression on her face is one of bewilderment. The metamorphosis into an animal is typical of Aztec imagery, and in Aztec symbolism the deer represents the right foot—the one that had been crushed in the accident so many years before. Kahlo painted this work right before she went to New York in 1946 to undergo a spinal fusion. She improved during her two months in the hospital, but her health grew worse on her return to Mexico. The spinal fusion seems to have marked the beginning of the inevitable decline that would lead to her death.

Kahlo underwent more than thirty operations to repair her broken body. From 1950 to her death, she spent most of her time flat on her back, often in the hospital. She never stopped painting—her easels were rigged to allow her to paint in bed or set at a height to allow her to paint from a wheelchair. *Self-Portrait with the Portrait of Doctor Farill* (1951) is the only painting in which Kahlo gives herself a painter's palette. Rather than paint on her palette, however, Kahlo displays her heart, and her brushes drip blood. The imagery recalls the Aztec sacrifices made to ensure the survival of the gods. It is through her painting that Kahlo managed to survive.

Final Triumphs

The Galería Arte Contemporáneo honored Kahlo with her first Mexican solo exhibition in May, 1953. Although her doctors forbade Kahlo to attend the opening, she arrived in an ambulance and held court from her four-poster bed in the middle of the gallery. She received the congratulations of her friends, sang *corridos* with them, and drank tequila until midnight. It was Frida's last triumph. The show was wildly successful, both in Mexico, where it was extended for a month, and among members of the international press, who acknowledged Kahlo's stature—not now as Rivera's wife but as an artist in her own right.

In August, 1953, the doctors decided that they had to amputate Frida's right leg because she had contracted gangrene. She never entirely regained her old zest for life after losing the leg. Although she continued to paint during the last year of her life, she lost the meticulous control of brushstroke and color that had characterized her work. She took drugs and alcohol to help her cope with pain, and they often caused her to behave erratically. Her moods would fluctuate swiftly from frantic gaiety to rage. The pages of her diary are full of surreal images of fantastic creatures and portents of death. She tried to stay connected with the life that was important to her—Diego, her painting, and her Communist convictions—but most of her days were bounded by the limitations of being an invalid. Although she was suffering from a case of pneumonia, she joined a Marxist demonstration protesting the overthrow of Guatemalan president Jacobo Arbenz Guzmá by a military regime supported by the Central Intelligence Agency. Less than two weeks later, on July 13, 1954, she died of a pulmonary embolism probably brought on by the pneumonia that she had made worse. The last words she wrote in her diary were:

I hope the exit is joyful—and I hope never to come back.
—*Frida*[31]

Chapter 10

Kahlo's Legacy

Kahlo's funeral was both fiesta and scandal. As soon as she died, her friends gathered at the Coyoacán house. They dressed her in a Tehuana skirt and white blouse and braided her hair with the customary ribbons and flowers. Diego was distraught and at first would talk to no one, but he did arrange with Andres Iduarte, Frida's old *cuate* from the National Preparatory School, then the director of the National Institute of Fine Arts, to have her body lie in state in the Palace of Fine Arts. Iduarte agreed, on condition that there would be no politics involved.

Although Rivera accepted Iduarte's condition, as soon as Frida's coffin was in place, one of Los Fridos, Arturo García Bustos, covered it with a red flag emblazoned with the Communist hammer and sickle. The honor guard that stood vigil over Frida's body included former president General Cárdenas, Frida's sisters, and prominent artists including David Siqueiros, Miguel Covarrubias, Juan O'Gorman, José Chávez Morado, and of course Diego. When the funeral procession carried Frida's coffin from the Palace of Fine Arts to the crematorium, five hundred mourners followed the hearse.

At the crematorium, Frida's friends gathered and sang revolutionary songs and ballads bidding her farewell. When her body was pulled into the fire, the heat made her sit up and her hair rose around her face in a dark halo. Four hours later, as her ashes emerged from the oven, they held, for a moment, the form of her skeleton. Diego quickly sketched his last glimpse of Frida, gathered her ashes in a red cloth, and put them into a cedar box. They remain in the Frida Kahlo Museum in Mexico City.

A Legacy Nearly Lost

As has happened with so many other women artists, even those who were admired and well known during their lives, Frida Kahlo's reputation began to fade after her death. Art historians have rarely focused on women's work, and so, despite the fact that Rivera had given the house in Coyoacán to the government of Mexico as the Frida Kahlo Museum, the knowledge of Kahlo's life and work began to disappear from the annals of art and even from the memory of Mexicans. It was the surge of feminist consciousness and the search for women artists in the 1970's and 1980's that brought Kahlo's work back into the mainstream of twentieth-century art.

Legacy Regained

The ground-breaking exhibition "Women Artists: 1550-1950," organized by Ann Sutherland Harris and Linda Nochlin, and its catalog published in 1981, challenged the traditional assumptions that women artists had existed only on the fringes of the art world and that their work did not deserve serious consideration by art scholars and historians. One of the artists included in the exhibition was Frida Kahlo.

In 1982, the Whitechapel Art Gallery in London mounted an exhibit of the photography of Tina Modotti and the paintings of Kahlo. The organizers of the exhibition wanted to show how Modotti's and Kahlo's works integrated art and politics, how each used popular images, and what their works reveal about the relationship between a personal, private world and the public sphere. Also in 1982, articles analyzing Kahlo's paintings began to appear in art journals.

A major biography of Kahlo by Hayden Herrera, published in 1983, became a best-seller and created international recognition for the artist. In response to the renewed interest and appreciation for Kahlo's work, the Mexican government declared her work to be part of the national heritage in 1984.

The dramatic quality of Kahlo's life also interested playwrights and filmmakers. A number of plays, films, and videos about her life and work were produced during the 1980's and 1990's. Even the rock star Madonna, who owns some works by Kahlo, has expressed an interest in portraying Kahlo in a film version of her life, saying: "She is my obsession and my inspiration."[32]

Museum visitors have also been given more opportunities to see Kahlo's work. In 1989 the Meadows Museum in Dallas presented an exhibition of sixty-three of her paintings. She was also included in a monumental exhibition called "Mexico: Splendors of Thirty Centuries," mounted by the Metropolitan Museum of Art in 1990, which traveled from New York to Los Angeles and San Antonio. Exhibitions of her work have also been mounted in Japan and Australia.

The market for the sale of Kahlo's work changed dramatically during the decade of the 1980's, reflecting her growing reputation. Kahlo's *Self-Portrait with Loose Hair* (1947), a painting that was valued at $15,000 in the early 1980's, sold for $1.65 million at an auction in 1991. The rediscovery of Frida Kahlo has led to a serious re-evaluation of her work that will be ongoing.

Kahlo's Artistic Legacy

When André Breton claimed Kahlo as an unconscious Surrealist, he was including her in one of the most influential art movements of the twentieth century. Breton's enthusiasm for Kahlo's work certainly helped her reputation and career, but she disdained the intellectual theories of the European Surrealists.

Kahlo's fantastic images arise more from her experience of life in Mexico—from the "magic" that reveals itself in the clash and integration of two very different cultures: the native Mexican (such as the Aztec and the Mayan) and the European.

What seems perfectly reasonable and rational to one culture has misunderstood "magical" powers to the other.

Some art critics have found Kahlo's extensive use of self-portraiture as a reason to consider her work less important. Such criticism reveals a double standard. Male artists, such as Rembrandt van Rijn and Albrecht Dürer, are praised for objective self-examination when they paint what they see in the mirror, but female artists are considered vain and self-absorbed when they paint their own portraits.

Kahlo's self-portraits explore the realities of being a Mexican, of being a woman, and of being crippled by both emotional and physical pain. Rivera said of her self-portraits: "Frida is the only example in the history of art of an artist who tore open her chest and heart to reveal the biological truth of her feelings . . . a superior painter and the greatest proof of the renaissance of the art in Mexico."[33] The work of Frida Kahlo leads the audience into a new understanding of how different cultures affect each other, of how ancient beliefs inform modern consciousness, and of how one artist attempted to "give birth to herself" and paint "the most wonderful poem of her life."[34]

Paintings

The following list of selected paintings are discussed in the text (asterisked) or are most readily available for public viewing; information is derived from Hayden Herrera's Frida Kahlo: The Paintings (New York: HarperCollins, 1991).

1926
*Self-Portrait, oil on canvas, 31″ × 23″
Private collection, Mexico City

1927
La Adelita, Pancho Villa, and Frida, oil on canvas, 25⅝″ × 17¾″
Instituto Tlaxcalteca de Cultura, Tlaxcala, Mexico

*Las Cachuchas, oil on canvas, 25⅝″ × 17¾″
Instituto Tlaxcalteca de Cultura, Tlaxcala, Mexico

1929
*The Bus, oil on canvas, 10¼″ × 22″
Dolores Olmedo Foundation, Mexico City

Portrait of Virginia (Niña), oil on Masonite, 33″ × 26⅘″
Dolores Olmedo Foundation, Mexico City

*Self-Portrait, oil on Masonite, 31¼″ × 27½″
Collection of Antony Bryan

1931
*Frida and Diego Rivera, oil on canvas, 39⅛″ × 31″
San Francisco Museum of Modern Art, California

*Luther Burbank, oil on Masonite, 34½″ × 24½″
Dolores Olmedo Foundation, Mexico City

*Portrait of Dr. Leo Eloesser, oil on Masonite, 33½″ × 23½″
University of California, San Francisco, School of Medicine

1932
Henry Ford Hospital, oil on metal, 12¼" × 15½"
Dolores Olmedo Foundation, Mexico City

My Birth, oil on metal, 12½" × 14"
Private collection, United States

Self-Portrait on the Border Line Between Mexico and the United States,
oil on metal, 12½" × 13¾"
Collection of Mr. and Mrs. Manuel Reyero, New York

1933
My Dress Hangs There, oil/collage on Masonite, 18" × 19¾"
Estate of Dr. Leo Eloesser, Hoover Gallery, San Francisco

1935
A Few Small Nips, oil on metal, 15" × 19"
Dolores Olmedo Foundation, Mexico City

1936
My Grandparents, My Parents, and I, oil/tempera on metal, 12⅛" × 13⅜"
Museum of Modern Art, New York

1937
The Deceased Dimas, oil on Masonite, 18⅞" × 12⅜"
Dolores Olmedo Foundation, Mexico City

Fulang-Chang and I, oil on composition board, 15¾" × 11"
Museum of Modern Art, New York

Me and My Doll, oil on metal, 15¾" × 12¼"
Jacques and Natasha Gelman Collection, Mexico City

Memory, oil on metal, 15¾" × 11"
Private collection, Paris

FRIDA KAHLO

My Nurse and I, oil on metal, 11¾" × 13¾"
Dolores Olmedo Foundation, Mexico City

Portrait of Diego Rivera, oil on wood, 18¹⁄₁₀" × 12½"
Jacques and Natasha Gelman Collection, Mexico City

Self-Portrait, Dedicated to Leon Trotsky, oil on Masonite, 30" × 24"
National Museum of Women in the Arts, Washington, D.C.

1938
Four Inhabitants of Mexico, oil on wood, 12¼" × 18¾"
Private collection, California

The Frame, oil on metal with glass, 11½" × 8½"
National Museum of Modern Art, Paris

Girl with Death Mask, oil on metal, 7⅘" × 5⅘"
Private collection, Monterrey, Mexico

Itzcuintli Dog with Me, oil on canvas, 11" × 8"
National Museum of Women in the Arts, Washington, D.C.

Self-Portrait with Monkey, oil on Masonite, 16" × 12"
Albright-Knox Art Gallery, Buffalo, New York

What the Water Gave Me, oil on canvas, 38" × 30"
Isadore Ducasse Fine Arts, New York

1939
The Suicide of Dorothy Hale, oil on Masonite, 23¼" × 19"
Phoenix Art Museum, Phoenix, Arizona

The Two Fridas, oil on canvas, 67" × 67"
Museo de Arte Moderno, Mexico City

Two Nudes in a Forest, oil on sheet metal, 9⅞" × 11⅞"
Mary-Anne Martin/Fine Arts, New York

THE ARTS

1940
The Dream, oil on canvas, 29¼" × 38¾"
Private collection, New York

Self-Portrait, oil on canvas, 24½" × 18¾"
Harry Ransom Humanities Research Center, University of Texas, Austin

Self-Portrait with Cropped Hair, oil on canvas, 15¾" × 11"
Museum of Modern Art, New York

*The Wounded Table, oil on canvas, 47⅘" × 96½"
Location unknown

1942
Self-Portrait with Monkey and Parrot, oil on Masonite, 21" × 17"
IBM Corporation, Armonk, New York

Still Life, oil on metal, 24⅘" in diameter
Frida Kahlo Museum, Mexico City

1943
The Bride Frightened at Seeing Life Opened, oil on canvas, 24⅘" × 32"
Jacques and Natasha Gelman Collection, Mexico City

Roots, oil on metal, 11¾" × 14½"
Private collection, Houston, Texas

1944
*The Broken Column, oil on Masonite, 15¾" × 12¼"
Dolores Olmedo Foundation, Mexico City

Diego and Frida 1929-1944, oil on wood, .9" × 2.9" (image), 10.2" × 7.2" (frame)
Collection of Manuel Arango, Mexico City

Flower of Life, oil on Masonite, 11½" × 9"
Dolores Olmedo Foundation, Mexico City

1945

The Mask, oil on Masonite, 15⅘" × 11⅘"
Dolores Olmedo Foundation, Mexico City

Moses, oil on Masonite, 37" × 20"
Private collection, Houston, Texas

Without Hope, oil on canvas, 11" × 14¼"
Dolores Olmedo Foundation, Mexico City

1946

*The Little Deer, oil on Masonite, 8⅞" × 11⅞"
Mary-Anne Martin/Fine Arts, New York

1947

*Self-Portrait with Loose Hair, oil on Masonite, 24" × 17¾"
Private collection, Mexico City

Sun and Life, oil on Masonite, 15¾" × 19½"
Private collection, Mexico City

1949

Diego and I, oil on Masonite, 11⅝" × 8¹³⁄₁₆"
Mary-Anne Martin/Fine Arts, New York

*The Love Embrace of the Universe, the Earth (Mexico), Diego, Me and
Señor Xolotl*, oil on canvas, 27½" × 23⅞"
Centro Cultural Arte Contemporaneo, Mexico City

1951

My Family, oil on Masonite, 16¹⁄₁₀" × 23⅕"
Frida Kahlo Museum, Mexico City

*Portrait of Don Guillermo Kahlo, oil on Masonite, 23⅘" × 18³⁄₁₀"
Frida Kahlo Museum, Mexico City

Self-Portrait with the Portrait of Doctor Farill, oil on Masonite, 16½" × 19¾"
Private collection, Mexico City

Still Life with Parrot, oil on canvas, 10" × 11"
Harry Ransom Humanities Research Center, University of Texas, Austin

1952
Naturaleza viva, oil on canvas
Galleria Arvil, Mexico City

1954
Fruit of Life, oil on Masonite, $17^{7}/_{10}$" × $24^{2}/_{5}$"
Private collection, Mexico City

Time Line

1907   Magdalena Carmen Frida Kahlo y Calderón is born on July 6 in Coyoacán, Mexico, to Matilde Calderón y González and Guillermo Kahlo.

1910   The Mexican Revolution erupts. Kahlo will claim this as her birth year in order to associate her own beginnings with the beginning of the Mexican Revolution.

1922   Kahlo enters the National Preparatory School in Mexico City.

1925   The collision of a bus with the trolley in which Kahlo is riding results in grave injuries from which she never fully recovers.

1926   Kahlo paints her first oil, *Self-Portrait Wearing a Velvet Dress*, while recuperating from the accident.

1927   Kahlo joins the Young Communist League.

1928   Kahlo receives encouragement from Diego Rivera to continue painting. He depicts her in *Distribution of Arms*, a fresco in the Ministry of Education.

1929   Diego Rivera and Frida Kahlo are married on August 21.

1930   Kahlo accompanies Rivera to San Francisco, where she meets Imogen Cunningham, Dr. Leo Eloesser, and Edward Weston.

1931   Kahlo's *Frida and Diego Rivera*, a wedding portrait, is exhibited at the Sixth Annual Exhibition of the San Francisco Society of Women Artists.

1932   Kahlo accompanies Rivera to Detroit, where she suffers a miscarriage. She begins to paint in *retablo* style and to record her life in paintings. Her mother dies.

1933   Kahlo accompanies Rivera to New York City, where he has been commissioned to paint a mural in Rockefeller Center. The commission is canceled after a political dispute. On their return to Mexico, Kahlo and Rivera move into the house at San Ángel.

1936   Kahlo and Rivera become involved in efforts to aid the Loyalist troops in the Spanish Civil War.

1937   Leon Trotsky arrives in Mexico and moves into the Riveras' house in Coyoacán. Kahlo's work is exhibited in a group exhibition at the Galería de Arte of the Department of Social Action, National Autonomous University of Mexico.

1938   Edward G. Robinson purchases four of Kahlo's paintings. Kahlo travels to New York for her first solo exhibit at the Julien Levy Gallery.

1939   Kahlo travels to Paris, where her work is featured in an exhibition entitled "Mexique" at the Galérie Pierre Colle. The Louvre purchases *The Frame*. Kahlo and Rivera are divorced.

1940   Kahlo's works are exhibited in the "International Exhibition of Surrealism" at the Galería de Arte Mexicano, in "Contemporary Mexican Painting and Graphic Art" in San Francisco, and in "Twenty Centuries of Mexican Art" at the Museum of Modern Art in New York. Kahlo and Rivera are remarried in San Francisco.

1941   Guillermo Kahlo dies. Kahlo's works are included in an exhibition entitled "Modern Mexican Painters" at the Institute of Contemporary Arts, Boston. She is selected as one of the founding members of the Seminaria de Cultura Mexicana by the Ministry of Education.

1942   Kahlo's works are included in the "Twentieth Century Portraits" exhibition at the Museum of Modern Art in New York and the "First Papers of Surrealism" exhibition sponsored by the Coordination of French Relief Societies.

1943   Kahlo is appointed as painting professor at La Esmeralda, the Ministry of Education's School of Painting and Sculpture. Because of her physical disabilities, she moves her classes to the Riveras' garden in Coyoacán. Her work is included in the exhibition "Thirty-one Women" at Peggy Guggenheim's Art of the Century Gallery in New York.

1946   Kahlo is awarded the National Prize of Arts and Sciences by the Ministry of Education. She travels to New York for a spinal fusion operation.

1950   Kahlo is hospitalized for a year following spinal surgery in Mexico.

1953   The Galería Arte Contemporáneo in Mexico City holds a solo exhibition of Kahlo's works. Kahlo's right leg is amputated.

1954   Eleven days after attending a political rally protesting the United States' intervention in Guatemala, Frida Kahlo dies on July 13 in Coyoacán.

Notes

Full bibliographic information may be found in the Bibliography, below.
1. Herrera, *Frida*, p. 11.
2. Herrera, *Paintings*, p. 24.
3. Herrera, *Frida*, p. 17.
4. Herrera, *Frida*, p. 18.
5. Press release from HarperCollins on Hayden Herrera's *Frida Kahlo: The Paintings*, 1991.
6. Herrera, *Frida*, p. 12.
7. Drucker, p. 7.
8. Herrera, *Paintings*, p. 23.
9. Herrera, *Frida*, p. 12.
10. Rivera and March, p. 129.
11. Wolfe, p. 241.
12. Herrera, *Frida*, pp. 50-51.
13. Rivera and March, p. 168.
14. Rivera and March, p. 172.
15. Herrera, *The Paintings*, p. 55.
16. Wolfe, pp. 247-248.
17. Translated by Herrera, *Paintings*, pp. 61-62.
18. Herrera, *Paintings*, p. 67.
19. Rivera and March, p. 172.
20. Rivera and March, p. 183.
21. Rivera and March, p. 202.
22. *Surrealism and Painting*, p. 144.
23. "Bomb Beribboned," November 14, 1938, p. 29.
24. Herrera, *Frida*, pp. 292-293.
25. Herrera, *Frida*, p. 252.
26. Herrera, *Frida*, pp. 245-246.
27. Wolfe, "Rise of Another Rivera," p. 64.
28. Herrera, *Frida*, p. 261.
29. "Mexican Autobiography," *Time*, April 27, 1953.
30. Herrera, *Frida*, p. 329.
31. Herrera, *Frida*, p. 431.
32. *Newsweek*, May 27, 1991, p. 54.
33. Herrera, *Paintings*, p. 4.
34. Herrera, *Paintings*, p. 9.

Glossary

Alegría: The love of life, a zest for living.

Anglo: A person of Northern European, usually English, descent. The term is often used by Latin Americans to describe North Americans.

Commission: The hiring of an artist by a patron (an individual, group, or government) to create an artwork, particularly for the patron. Sometimes the patron chooses the subject of the work or sets specifications for its completion.

Corrido: A narrative folk ballad in rhymed four-line stanzas; Mexico's outstanding contribution to American folk music and folk poetry.

Créole: A person of pure European descent who was born and reared in Mexico.

Cubism: A movement in modern art, which is more concerned with geometric forms than with the lifelike representation of Realism or the emphasis on light and color effects of Impressionism. Cubism drew inspiration from African and Oceanic tribal art. In a Cubist painting, the artist concentrates on the basic geometric shapes of the subject or simultaneously presents the subject from different angles.

Ex-voto or *retablo*: A small devotional painting offering thanks to a divine being, usually to the Virgin Mary, for delivery from danger or misfortune. In the painting, usually done on tin plates in Mexico, both the disastrous event and the divine being are depicted. A scrolled inscription describing the event, its date, and the people involved is included within the painting.

Magical Realism: A literary and artistic movement, first associated with Latin American artists, which combines elements of realism and the seemingly fantastic to illuminate the effects of different cultures and cultural expectations coming into contact with each other.

Mestizo: A Mexican of mixed European and Native American descent.

Mural: A large painting on a wall. Usually the muralist paints onto wet plaster so the paint becomes part of the plaster. The muralist movement in Mexico, begun in 1920 with the inauguration of Álvaro Obregón as president, produced the greatest public revolutionary art of the twentieth century.

No hay remedio: Literally, "There is no recourse." This was Kahlo's characteristic expression of the necessity of coping with her suffering and pain.

Pedregal: A rocky, volcanic expanse that is characteristic of some of the Mexican landscape. Kahlo often uses it as background in her paintings to indicate her close connection to the land.

La Pelona: A bald or stupid woman; the nickname Kahlo used to describe death.

Pre-Columbian: The term used to describe the peoples and cultures of the Americas before the landing of Christopher Columbus in 1492. In Mexico, the most important pre-Columbian cultures were the Aztec, the Maya, the Toltec, and the Olmec.

Realism: A movement in art and literature which attempts to present figures and objects exactly as they appear in life. When it refers to the art movement, the term generally describes the art of the nineteenth century, which began in reaction to the highly subjective stance of the Romantic movement.

Recuerdo: A memorial portrait to commemorate the death of a loved one. Kahlo's painting, *The Suicide of Dorothy Hale*, might be considered a *recuerdo*, although it has some characteristics of an *ex-voto*.

Surrealism: A movement in art and literature founded in Paris in 1924 by poet and critic André Breton with the publication of his *Surrealist Manifesto*. Surrealism emphasized the role of the unconscious and dream imagery in creative activity. As an organized movement, it remained under the leadership of Breton, but many artists—including Salvador Dalí, Pablo Picasso, Joan Miró, and Frida Kahlo—moved in and out of the structured group while incorporating Surrealist techniques and ideas into their works.

Bibliography

Breton, André. *Surrealism and Painting*. Translated by Simon Watson
Taylor. New York: Harper & Row, 1972. Breton's book on Surrealist
painting contains the essay he wrote for the exhibition brochure for
Kahlo's show at the Julien Levy Gallery in New York in 1938.

Drucker, Malka. *Frida Kahlo: Torment and Triumph in Her Life and Art*.
Introduction by Laurie Anderson. New York: Bantam, 1991. A
biography of Frida Kahlo written as introduction to the artist's life and
work. It focuses particularly on the transmutation of her pain into art. As
the first in the Barnard Biography Series of heroic women, the level of
writing is accessible to a young adult audience.

Frida Kahlo: Posterbook. Text by Jutta Koether. English translation by
Michael Hulse. Berlin: Taschen, 1991. A collection of six large-format
(31-by-44-centimeter) glossy prints of Kahlo paintings, with critical
commentary in German, French, and English on each of the paintings.
The paintings, reprinted by permission of the Instituto Nacional de
Bellas Artes, Mexico City, include *Frida Kahlo and Diego Rivera*
(1931), *Self-Portrait with Monkey* (1938), *The Suicide of Dorothy Hale*
(1938-1939), *Self-Portrait for Dr. Eloesser* (1940), *The Broken Column*
(1944), and *Flag of Hope* (1946).

Frida Kahlo: The Camera Seduced. San Francisco: Lookout/Chronicle,
1992. Sixty pictures by such photographers as Edward Weston, Imogen
Cunningham, Ansel Adams, Lucienne Bloch, and Manuel Alvarez
Bravo. The text includes a fictional memoir by Elena Poniatowska and
an essay by Carla Stellweg.

Herrera, Hayden. *Frida: A Biography of Frida Kahlo*. New York: Harper &
Row, 1983. Herrera wrote the first major biography of Kahlo, and it
remains the standard work on her life. The publication of this biography
reawakened interest in Kahlo's art and was responsible for a revival of
her reputation.

_____ . *Frida Kahlo: The Paintings*. New York: HarperCollins,
1991. This bountiful collection of Kahlo's paintings and drawings
(eighty-three color reproductions, seventy-four black-and-white
reproductions) is accompanied by more than one hundred photographs
and a biographical analysis. The paintings are beautifully presented in
full-page reproductions: Kahlo's face stares out at and challenges the
viewer on page after page.

Jenkins, Nicholas. "Calla Lilies and Kahlos." *ARTnews* (March, 1991): 104-105. A guided tour through the Frida Kahlo Museum in Mexico City.

Lowe, Sarah M. *Frida Kahlo*. New York: Universe, 1991. A scholarly monograph on Frida Kahlo which contains a brief biographical overview. The discussion of Kahlo's painting focuses on her self-portraits, her connections to the Surrealist movement, her "primitivistic" techniques, and an examination of her still-lifes.

Plagens, Peter, et al. "Frida on Our Minds." *Newsweek* (May 27, 1991): 54-55. An article instigated by the sale of Kahlo's painting *Self-Portrait with Loose Hair* for $1.65 million, it investigates "Frida fever" as it has manifested itself in the many films, books, and sales of her paintings during the late 1980's and early 1990's.

Rivera, Diego, with Gladys March. *My Art, My Life: An Autobiography*. New York: Citadel, 1960. Rivera dictated this autobiography (one of four that have been published) to March. It is the standard autobiography in English and contains Rivera's versions of his life with Kahlo and some discussion of her work.

Whitechapel Art Gallery. *Frida Kahlo and Tina Modotti*. Exhibition catalog. London: Whitechapel Art Gallery, 1982. The exhibition mounted at Whitechapel Art Gallery included paintings by Kahlo and photographs by Modotti. The essay by Laura Mulvey and Peter Wollen focuses on the revolutionary and feminist aspects of each woman's work. Other appreciations included are by Diego Rivera, Carleton Beals, Martí Casanovas, Pablo Neruda, André Breton, and Alejandro Gómez Arias.

Wolfe, Bertram D. *The Fabulous Life of Diego Rivera*. 2d rev. ed. 1963. Reprint. New York: Stein & Day, 1984. Bertram Wolfe and his wife, Ella, were close friends of Diego Rivera and Frida Kahlo. This second edition of his biography of Rivera is a complete revision of the 1939 edition and includes details of the period from 1939 to Rivera's death in 1957. The biography includes information about the Rivera-Kahlo marriage, much of it supplied by Kahlo, as the author acknowledges in his introduction.

Zamora, Martha. *Frida Kahlo: The Brush of Anguish*. Abridged and translated by Marilyn Sode Smith. San Francisco: Chronicle Books, 1990. The English version of Zamora's book is taken up mostly with color reproductions of many of Kahlo's paintings and a good selection of photographs of the artist. The text is mainly biographical.

Media Resources

Crommie, Karen, and David Crommie. *The Life and Death of Frida Kahlo as Told to David and Karen Crommie*. Documentary film. 1976. Contains interviews with friends and associates of Kahlo. Coupled with images of the artist and her canvases, this documentary traces the life and work of Kahlo.

Leduc, Paul. *Frida*. Film (available on video), 108 minutes. 1984. Video distributed by Facets Multimedia. A visual tribute to Kahlo, told in surrealistic flashbacks reminiscent of Kahlo's paintings. With Ofelia Medina, Juan José Gurrola, and Max Kerlow. Spanish dialogue with English subtitles.

Lo, Louise. *Frida Kahlo: Portrait of an Artist*. Documentary film. Narrated by Edward James Olmos. Pittsburgh, Pa.: PBS/KQED, 1988. Includes archival films of Kahlo and Rivera, still photos, taped interviews with friends, and examples of Kahlo's and Rivera's paintings.

Mandel, Ken, Jeff Hurst, and Cora Cardona. *Frida Kahlo: A Ribbon Around a Bomb*. Film, 71 minutes. 1992. Distributed by Roxie. A performance film that weaves together interviews with people who knew Kahlo, photographs and films of her and many of her paintings, and excerpts of a theater piece, *The Diary of Frida Kahlo*, by Abraham Oceransky, as performed by Cora Cardona and Quigley Provost at the Teatro Dallas.

RM Arts/Hershon Guerra/WDR. *Frida Kahlo: Portrait of an Artist*. Video, 62 minutes. 1983. Distributed by Home Vision. A look at the life and work of Kahlo narrated by Sada Thompson with commentary by Hayden Herrera.

INDEX

Madonna, 92
Marín, Lupe, 26, 43
Marriage to Diego Rivera, 37-43, 73
Marxism. *See* Communism.
Maternal grandparents, 22
Meadows Museum, 92
Metropolitan Museum of Art, 92
Mexican culture in Kahlo's art, 11-18
Mexican Revolution, 11-13, 14, 15, 20
Mexicanidad movement, 13-14
"Mexico: Splendors of Thirty Centuries," 92
Modotti, Tina, 35, 45, 91
Muray, Nickolas, 41, 78, 81
My Art, My Life, 26
My Birth, 14
My Dress Hangs There, 67
My Grandparents, My Parents, and I, 21
My Nurse and I, 14-16

National Preparatory School, 26-30
Nevelson, Louise, 78
New York City, 67-69, 78-79
Noguchi, Isamu, 41, 78

O'Keeffe, Georgia, 78

Painting, as a response to her accident, 33
Paris, France, 80-81
Pedregal, 22
Pelona, 32-33
Photography, 23
Popularity of Kahlo's art, 91

Portrait of Don Guillermo Kahlo, 24
Pre-Columbian art, 16, 66

Rabel, Fanny, 83
Rebozo, 40, 46
Recuerdo, 78
Retablo, 14
Rivera, Diego, 26-28, 35-36; affairs with other women, 41-43; divorce and remarriage to Kahlo, 85-86; influence on Kahlo's art, 38-39; marriage to Kahlo, 37-43, 73
Robinson, Edward G., 74
Rockefeller, Nelson, 67, 78
Rockefeller Center, 67-69

San Ángel, 73, 86
San Francisco, California, 44-48
Schiaparelli, Giovanni, 81
Self-Portrait (1929), 39-40
Self-Portrait on the Border Line Between Mexico and the United States, 66-67
Self-Portrait with Loose Hair, 92
Self-Portrait with the Portrait of Doctor Farill, 88
Self-portraiture, women vs. men, 94
Soldaderas, 46
Spanish Civil War, 71, 81
Stalin, Joseph, 41, 70
Stieglitz, Alfred, 78
Suicide of Dorothy Hale, The, 78-79
Surgeries, 31-36, 88-89
Surrealism, 75-78, 80-82, 92

Teaching, 83-85
Tehuana costume, 45-46

Teotihuacán culture, 16
Trotsky, Leon, 41, 70-71, 75, 85;
    assassination of, 85
Trotsky, Natalia, 71

United States trip (1930-1933),
    44-48, 65-69

Vasconcelos, José, 28, 35

Weston, Edward, 46
What the Water Gave Me, 73, 76
Whitechapel Art Gallery, 91
Women artists, 91
"Women Artists: 1550-1950," 91

Young Communist League, 35

Zapata, Emiliano, 13